SEP 2 2 2007

THE LACROSSE TRAINING BIBLE

THE COMPLETE GUIDE FOR MEN AND WOMEN

Vincent Perez-Mazzola

with contributions by
Matt Brown

Foreword by
Jamie Mu
Head Coach, Men's
University of Denver

HatherleighPress

New York • London

HatherleighPress
5-22 46th Avenue, Suite 200
Long Island City, NY 11101
www.hatherleighpress.com

DISCLAIMER
Before beginning any exercise program, consult your physician. The author and the publisher disclaim any liability, personal or professional, resulting from the application or misapplication of any of the information in this publication.

Library of Congress Cataloging-in-Publication Data

Perez-Mazzola, Vincent.
 The lacrosse training bible : the complete guide for men and women /
Vincent Perez-Mazzola ; contributions from Matt Brown.
     p. cm.
 Includes bibliographical references and index.
 ISBN-13: 978-1-57826-249-6
 1. Lacrosse—Training. I. Brown, Matt. II. Title.
 GV989.15.P47 2007
 796.34'7—dc22

                        2007016607

The Lacrosse Training Bible is available for bulk purchase, special promotions, and premiums. For information on reselling and special purchase opportunities, call 1-800-528-2550 and ask for the Special Sales Manager.

Special thanks to: **Maximum Fitness**, 8551 E. Anderson Dr., Scottsdale, AZ 85255

Interior design by Jasmine Cardoza
Cover design by Deborah Miller, Allison Furrer, Jasmine Cardoza
Photos by Chris Loomis (www.chrisloomis.com) unless otherwise noted
Thanks to our models: Austin B. Gray, Jessica Livingston, Kyle Kingsbury, Liza Lipson

10 9 8 7 6 5 4 3 2 1

Printed in Canada

Dedication

To Coach Young and Professor Lawrence for teaching me the game.
To Albin and all the Arizona Youth Lacrosse Players for bringing me back to the game.
And to all players past, present, and future that continue to grow the game.

Special thanks to "Uncle" Phil for making this book possible.

Table of Contents

FOREWORD

Lacrosse is the fastest-growing sport in the United States, but what might surprise you is how closely it is tied to other mainstream sports. In my position as head coach of the University of Denver's men's lacrosse team, I've had to direct my boys' movements, and sometimes the easiest way is to draw the parallel between lacrosse and football, basketball, soccer, hockey, and even tennis.

There is so much crossover between the skill sets of team sports. For example, a give and go works in soccer, basketball, and hockey as well as it does in lacrosse. Soccer has its footwork, stamina, field vision, spacing, off-ball movement. Basketball has 1-on-1 defensive and offensive skills as well as team defensive and offensive skills, the pick-and-roll game, passing, as well as man-to-man and zone concepts. Football is unmatched for pure athletic skills, and if you watch closely, the footwork is the same between the offensive lineman and defensive as it is in 1-on-1 lacrosse. Hockey has passing, scrapping for a puck, odd man situations, and anticipation. Even an individual sport like tennis, if you look at how a player holds his racket, can teach you valuable skills that will help you become a better lacrosse player.

So, how do you train for a sport that combines so many elements of several sports into one? There's many things that intrigue me about the game of lacrosse, but none more than the development of its players. I believe player development and self-improvement is an exciting process as well as a rewarding one and can easily be broken down into three categories: athletic skills, individual skills, and team concepts.

Athletic skill is your strength, speed, footwork, and explosiveness. There many ways to train for this, such as lifting weights, running drills, and plyometrics, all covered later in *The Lacrosse Training Bible*. I encourage you to make sure you are under the supervision of a coach or trainer who knows what they're doing, because injury is a real possibility.

Individual skills are your stick skills, dodging, feeding, cutting, and shooting skills. I recommend you begin your practice watching pro lacrosse players, both indoor and outdoor and start to emulate the best in the world. If you're picking up a stick for the very first time, you should start with drill after drill—how to catch, throw, dodge, cradle, field ground balls, pass, and shoot. Getting these basic skills down to where they are instinctive with no hesitation can take a long time, but is rewarding in the end. You'll find some drills in the pages to come, but don't let these be the only things you attempt.

If I had to point out the single most important technique for developing individual skills, it would be to play with your lefties on the right (looking at the cage) and your righties on the left. The reason is simple: it allows a player to attack the middle of the field to his strong hand while dodging top side or underneath. Attackmen naturally play on their proper side, but middies and defensemen usually run to the wrong side of the field. I learned this lesson watching Canadians play box lacrosse. The goals are so much smaller that if one does not dodge with his stick to the middle, there will be not enough angle to score.

I believe attackmen are usually more skilled players than midfielders for this reason: they learn more skills from playing on their proper side. The midfielder learns to run down the side to his strong hand and learns to shoot, feed, or pass. The attackman learns to dodge to the middle of the field top side or underneath, and a variety of moves that can include inside rolls, pop outs, question mark moves, rocker steps, and many more.

The same concept holds true off the ball. The midfielder usually cuts down the alley stick to the outside, losing angle with every step, whereas the attackman learns to cut the middle either top side of his man or underneath his man gaining precious angle with every step.

Team concepts are the elements to the game involving the offense and defense as a whole six versus six offense/defense as well as rides/clears and EMO/EMD. It's quite possible that the best way to learn these concepts is not by playing and watching just lacrosse, but by expanding your vision to include other team sports, like football or soccer. I do of course suggest watching as much college lacrosse as possible to see just how the offenses attack and the defenses defend. When you do that, you'll notice the offense swings the ball from one side of the field to the other because the defense clogs up the ball side.

Training to play lacrosse will be challenging, mentally and physically. If you've picked up *The Lacrosse Training Bible* in the off-season, you're giving yourself a head start for the season ahead. Remember, while there is only so much you can do without your team by your side, by yourself, you can do quite a lot. You can grow quicker, stronger, more agile, and drill dodges, rushes, checks, and throwing. Your stick skills certainly won't suffer for practice, and that will be extremely valuable to your team.

In the following pages, you'll find many ways to work hard at your athletic and individual skills, but it's up to you how much time you want to dedicate to this sport, definitely the fastest on two feet.

Good luck.

—Jamie Munro
Head Coach, Men's Lacrosse, University of Denver

INTRODUCTION

HOW TO USE THIS BOOK

This book is designed to be used by players, coaches, trainers, and lacrosse enthusiasts. Its goal is to provide a comprehensive guidebook for anyone desiring to prepare for and play the great game of lacrosse at a competitive level. It provides a step-by-step approach to the fundamentals of the game both in skill development and in athletic training.

You do not have to be a Division 1 lacrosse player to use this book. Indeed, it is aimed more specifically at people still at the beginning levels of the game. The book is written by a former player and current coach, with generous input from many coaches and players including the pros. There are more than 50 years of accumulated lacrosse experience distilled in this book. My goal is to provide you with information that will further your personal goals as a player and also promote the development of the game we love.

The book is divided into both informational and practical sections. The former explain the evolution of the modern game, examine its current state, and look to likely future developments. The latter provides step-by-step, cutting-edge training methods to turn lacrosse athletes into champions. The training chapters are formatted like a lesson/practice plan, for ease of use by coaches or by players pursuing off-season training on their own. It is important to note that many of the training methods used in this book may conflict with traditional methods. This is done on purpose, in order to yank lacrosse training out of the dark ages and into the highly specialized world of functional athletic training. Too long have lacrosse players been persuaded or forced to train using archaic methods. Our sport deserves more than that, and with the advent of a new professionalism in sports training, it is time that twenty-first century methods be applied to the way in which we learn and teach lacrosse.

The training chapters in this book are subdivided into sections that are meant to be both simple to follow and largely self-contained. We begin with an examination of the proper core warm-up, followed immediately by a program for agility training. Strength, speed, and balance come next, setting out the heart of the lacrosse conditioning program. Workouts are tailored to different times of the lacrosse season: post-, pre-, and in-season. The conditioning sections of this book offer cutting-edge methods to prepare you to play this physically demanding game. It is strongly recommended that you follow the conditioning programs presented, completely and in the order presented, before you launch into serious skills training.

After conditioning you to play the game, the book turns to the skills of the game. Cradling, fielding, catching, throwing, passing, shooting, and dodging each has its own chapter. Many of the skill drills contained in these chapters are exercises to be digested and practiced now and throughout your lacrosse career. Again, it is recommended that you work on these skills in the order presented. You will understand why as your game develops.

After the basic skills of the game, we turn to skills and tactics that are critical to the position you will play. Everyone on the field is both a defender and offensive player to some degree, but the goalie, defenders, midfielders, and attackmen all must master the special skills of their positions. Learn the basics of all the positions, and let your natural talents and instincts choose your place on the field.

For current players, this part of the book can help you reinvent yourself as a player and athlete. Always remember that this book is not a strict set of rules to live and play by, but only a guide that should be utilized to provide a base of athleticism and competence. Each person is free to and expected to take and develop what is presented here to another level.

Supplementing and reinforcing the author's training program, we are privileged to have tips and information from lacrosse star Matt Brown. A former star collegiate player for the University of Denver, this Canadian native has played professional lacrosse both indoors, with the National Lacrosse League (Arizona Sting) and out on the field with Major League Lacrosse (Denver Outlaws). As a player, coach and equipment distributor Matt brings with him the cutting-edge knowledge and ability of this rapidly growing sport. Use his insights and tips to further illuminate the drills contained within this book.

Best of luck on your journey.

2005 NCAA Women's Lacrosse Championship game where the Virginia Cavaliers lost to the Northwestern University Wildcats

PART I

HISTORY OF THE GAME

This oil painting was completed in the mid-1800s and entitled "Ball-play of the Choctaw—Ball Up," and depicted Native Americans playing lacrosse.

CHAPTER 1

NATIVE AMERICAN ORIGINS AND EVOLUTION OF THE MODERN GAME

NATIVE AMERICAN ORIGINS

Lacrosse is an exciting game, and once upon a time it may have been even more exciting, Native American tribes originated and played it for centuries before the European came. There are reports of it being played as far back as the 1400's. Native Americans in eastern Canada and the Northeastern United States called the game Bagataway or Tekwaarathon. Hundreds of Native Americans often took the field in two teams and sometimes played all day. Bloody scrimmages often aimed to disable the defenders rather than outmaneuver them. Serious casualties were expected. It was considered a right of passage for young men, and spiritually linked to many aspects of Native American culture. It was sometimes even an agreed upon substitute for a war between tribes. Native Americans called lacrosse the "little brother of war" because of these bloody intertribal showdowns. Modern box lacrosse games are exciting and notoriously rough contests, but still a far cry from the "little war" games of the Iroquois!

As an integral part of Native American culture, as we said, it was also more than just a game or contest. It was a reflection of Native American society and spirituality as a whole. Seen as a gift from the Almighty, it was often referred to as the "Creators Game," and was therefore an appropriate instrument to settle disputes, heal the sick, and train young warriors in preparation for war.

Among the Native American people many versions of the game were played, sometimes using teams of a few select warriors to teams of an entire village. The more progressive tribes even allowed women and men to compete on the same teams, though women typically played their own form of the sport, as they do to this day. The contestants played on fields of varying dimensions, from a few hundred feet to over 12 miles in length with goals situated at either end. The games could last for days and days, and as we said, serious injuries were expected. Since most players on the field of that size never got near the ball, they apparently decided to concentrate on using their sticks to injure opponents, taking them out of the game by using their sticks as bludgeons. Early European visitors were shocked by how bloody and brutal an affair it was.

Historic evidence shows us that each tribe used their own unique form of lacrosse stick. Sticks were made out of natural fibers and materials such as wood, deerskin, and leather. So important was the stick to the culture that is was thought to somehow establish a spiritual connection to all players of the game on this earth and beyond. The sticks when fashioned held great personal importance to the owner and reflected the strength and character of the tribe as well. Great respect was given to the stick itself and it was never to be left uncared for or abused. Like the sword carried by Samurai warriors, the lacrosse stick embodied the spirit of the game and the warrior who played it.

Winning the modern game remains, as it did in tribal times, a function of scoring goals by placing the ball against or though a structure that we now call a goal. Some tribes used a single pole, tree, or rock for a goal, while others had two goalposts through which the ball had to pass, much like today's goalposts. The balls themselves were made out of many different materials such as wood, stuffed deerskin, baked clay, or even stone. Though there was less passing of the ball than there is today, getting hit by one of these tribal balls was probably as unhealthy as getting hit by the stick. No protective equipment was ever worn. Lacrosse was truly a game of survival of the fittest.

One of the largest groups of Native Americans to play lacrosse was, and still is, The Six Nations federation of tribes. The Six Nations is a coalition

LACROSSE sticks today are high-tech gadgets made out of metal alloys and plastic. However, the old wooden sticks of Native American times can still be had. Indeed, they remain an important part of Native American heritage; many Native American players still keep true to the old ways and play with the heavier sticks made of wood and leather. As living pieces of indigenous culture and history, a hand-carved lacrosse stick is a thing of beauty and utmost craftsmanship. And since it is made by hand, no two sticks are alike. Today Mohawk International Lacrosse is the last remaining Native American manufacturer of lacrosse sticks. Located on the Akwesasne Reservation, MIL continues a tradition begun many years ago by the Mohawk people who have played the game of lacrosse since the 1500s.

that includes the Mohawks, Oneidas, Onondagas, Cayugas, Senecas, and Tuscaroras. These federation tribes were the first peoples to live under a written constitution and are considered by historians to be the oldest living participatory democracy on earth. Their system of governance was an inspiration and guide to our nation's own founding fathers and framers of the Constitution.

THE DEVELOPMENT OF THE GAME

The development from a Native American ritual to a modern sport began in 1636, when a Jesuit missionary named Jean de Brebeuf documented a lacrosse game played by the Huron in what is now southeast Ontario, Canada. He was amazed to find that some form of the game was being played by at least 48 Native American tribes scattered throughout southern Canada and all parts of the United States. A standardization and development of one set of accepted rules and regulations would not take place until two hundred years later, when French pioneers began regularly playing a form of the game. Then, later in the nineteenth century, other Europeans in Canada also began playing and eventually the first organized team of non-Native Americans was formed.

OH, CANADA

The adoption of the game by Canadian settlers marked a turning point in the history of the sport. The new colonists took to the native game and added rules and regulations in an attempt to standardize and codify the sport. The key player in this transition was a Canadian dentist named W. George Beers, credited by many as the founder of modern lacrosse. Though a dentist by profession, Beers was an avid lacrosse fan and player, who as an original member of the Montreal Lacrosse Club rewrote the rules thoroughly in 1867. The newly modernized rules called for each side to field a team of 12 players playing defined positions. The positions were goal, point, cover point, first defense, second defense, third defense, centre, third attack, second attack, first attack, out home, and in home.

Beers also updated the equipment for modern play, manufacturing a hard rubber ball, and designing a stick that was better suited to catching and throwing than the native sticks, which were designed more to carry the ball. With new rules and equipment there soon came new techniques for throwing, catching, and shooting the ball, as well as strategies and techniques for more structured team play.

Canada's National Lacrosse Association, also established in 1867, quickly adopted Beers' new rulebook. In that same year, a team made up of Caughnawaga Indians traveled to England and played an exhibition match for Queen Victoria. The British were immediately quite taken with this import from the colonies. Teams sprang up in areas such as Bristol, Cheshire, Lancashire, London, Manchester, and Yorkshire. This grass-roots development of the game led to the establishment of the English Lacrosse Union, organized in 1892. Though interest in the sport waned between the wars, lacrosse is still being played in England by thousands of young women and is now once again catching on with men.

THE MODERN GAME

The sport of lacrosse is to most observers a combination of basketball, soccer, and hockey. The skill set is more varied than in any other sport, so much so that virtually anyone can play and do well in some part of the game. Lacrosse is also flexible enough to be open to personal interpretation and style. For example, a larger stronger player will use power moves to get to the goal, while a smaller

Richmond Hill "Young Canadians" lacrosse team.

more agile player will use speed and deception. No matter your physical size, the ability to "see the field" and react quickly are great assets in lacrosse. This goes for both the men and women's game.

Though played differently, both men and women's lacrosse, and both indoor and outdoor versions, share a common ancestry from the Native American game. The split between the Canadian proclivity for the indoor game and the American love of the field game dominates the modern history of the common game. In the United States the first college to field a team was New York University in 1877. At the preparatory school level, Philips Academy, Andover (Massachusetts), Philips Exeter Academy (New Hampshire), and the Lawrenceville School (New Jersey) were the first to field teams around 1882. These well-endowed institutions still play the game today and have developed a legacy of lacrosse history. The first women's lacrosse team in America was begun at the Bryn Mawr School in Baltimore, Maryland in 1926.

The 1930s brought the Canadian lacrosse game back in from the cold as both the Native American game and the new American game of hockey were combined. This new indoor version of the game was born on the thawed hockey rinks of Canada and renamed box lacrosse or boxla for short. The modern version of the game was a high-impact demonstration of speed and action and very quickly won massive support within Canadian lacrosse organizations. By the mid-1930s the field game had been all but completely replaced by the box version of the game. Today the Canadian Lacrosse Association recognizes four separate disciplines of the game: Box, Men's Field, Women's Field, and Inter-Lacrosse. Box lacrosse still remains almost uniquely a Canadian devotion, though it is gradually beginning to catch on down "south of the boarder" with the appearance of the action-packed National Lacrosse League. The NLL offers year-round lacrosse played even in such hotter climes as Texas, Arizona, and California. In Canada, box lacrosse is appreciated as a highly physical game based on toughness and lightning-fast stickwork, while the field version of the game is seen as a sport of patience and strategy that focuses on control of the ball. The Canadians prefer their indoor version to America's field play, though the lines of distinction are beginning to blur.

Canada continues to provide the world with some of the most skilled players in the world. Born to the indoor arenas of box lacrosse, recruited to the States, and placed on the field, the Canadians bring with them a complete lacrosse experience that is beginning to make an impact in both the professional indoor and outdoor leagues. It is this mixed venue experience that arguably produces the best lacrosse players in the world.

It was not until the mid-1930s that the rules for men's and women's lacrosse began to evolve separately and develop into the very different games they are today. The men's game became more physical, allowing for both stick and body checks. To reduce injury, the development of protective equipment also proceeded at pace with the game. On the other hand, the women's game remained "civilized," with little stick-to-stick contact and virtually no body checking allowed at all. Some purists consider the women's game to be more like the original sport, though many wounded Native American warriors would not have agreed. To some people watching lacrosse for the first time, a game in which people hit, slash, and shoot with a stick and a hard ball, it may seem to have evolved very little from its combative roots. But in fact the sophisticated design of modern equipment, the fitness levels of the players, and the discipline of players have made this contact sport amazingly safe to play. A recent study ranked lacrosse as one of the least injurious of team sports played at any level. With this level of action, fun, and safety, it is no wonder lacrosse is catching on like wildfire.

> "LACROSSE is one of the fastest-growing team sports in the United States. Youth membership (ages 15 and under) in US Lacrosse has more than tripled since 1999 to nearly 100,000. No sport has grown faster at the high school level over the last 10 years and there are now more than 130,000 high school players. Lacrosse is also the fastest-growing sport over the last five years at the NCAA level and that's just the tip of the iceberg. There are more than 500 college club programs, the majority of which compete under the umbrella of U.S. Lacrosse and its "intercollegiate associates" level. Currently there are approximately 400 college and 1,200 high school men's lacrosse teams in the United States. This is just the tip of the iceberg numbers wise due to the unprecedented growth of youth lacrosse programs in the United States."
> ©US Lacrosse

CHAPTER 2

LACROSSE TODAY: FROM PROS TO YOUTH LEAGUES

The game of lacrosse has grown tremendously over the past few years. Since 1999 the number of high school and college players has exploded. Growing at a rate of 10 percent per year, lacrosse is on the brink of breaking out of regional popularity and onto the national and even world stage. Reebok, Nike, Toyota, Dodge, and New Balance have embraced the game with promotional deals, equipment, and more. ESPN and ESPN2 have signed contracts to broadcast outdoor collegiate and professional games, and the NCAA Division 1 Men's Tournament is the second most- attended college sports event after college basketball's March Madness. The Lacrosse World Games, which take place every four years, have grown to 22 teams from all over the globe. Nevertheless, most people's exposure to lacrosse is still local. Youth lacrosse leagues are popping up all over the nation, and men's club teams keep the game alive for the older generation.

The incredible growth of lacrosse is due to many factors: transplanted East Coasters moving out West and bringing their love for the game with them, the development of youth lacrosse leagues in the western states, and a general need for a new and exciting game to be enjoyed and played by the entire family. Lacrosse is also a sport that appeals to both men and women. Men may prefer a highly physical version of the game that maintains a lot of contact, while women prefer a version that is more skill-based, using less physicality and slightly different equipment. Nonetheless, both enjoy and play a game that is still lacrosse. It is not uncommon to see brother and sister or mom and dad, throwing the ball around together. This universal appeal has also helped to spur on lacrosse's development into a nation-wide craze.

As a spectator sport, lacrosse is an easy game to get hooked on. Even if you don't know all the rules, the hard checks, the fast runs, the high scores, and the physical play keeps you on the edge of your seat. This fan-friendly sport has spurred the founding of teams beyond the college spectrum and into the realm of professional athletics. The development of professional lacrosse leagues is not exactly news. The professional indoor league has been around for 20 years. What is new is the incredible success of these teams in non-traditional lacrosse areas of the nation. For example, in Denver, Colorado, the National Lacrosse League indoor team, the Mammoth, sells out every one of its 11,000 seats every game. So successful has the Denver market been that it has spurred the addition of a professional outdoor team, the Denver Outlaws. The newly constructed multi-million dollar Peter Barton Lacrosse stadium is the home field for the University of Denver Pioneers, who have shaken up the collegiate lacrosse world by becoming a western team that can compete and win at the Division 1 level.

As we said, the game of lacrosse diverged into two strong venues, the indoor rinks of box lacrosse in Canada and the East Coast fields of the United States. Both games lend handily to the sport as a whole. The recent interest in lacrosse as a sport has allowed both versions to flourish and develop professional leagues that offer excitement and fun to players and fans alike. The indoor game gives National Hockey League venues options for filling the stands while their NHL team is on the road and has helped to increase revenue for many franchise owners.

THE NATIONAL LACROSSE LEAGUE

Based out of New York City, the National Lacrosse League has been in existence since 1986. Originally called the Eagle Box Lacrosse League, and then the Major Indoor Lacrosse League, it was the brainchild of two former lacrosse players, Chris Fritz and Russ Kline. The initial years of indoor lacrosse were marred by a lack of interest in the game and an unusual marketing campaign that included players wearing spandex shorts as part of their unique uniforms. The games were action-packed and sometimes violent, to the delight of the roughneck hockey fans to which they typically played. In 1997, the league changed names and became the National Lacrosse League we know now. Due to an aggressive and organized marketing campaign, the NLL has expanded aggressively in the United States.

As the national sport of Canada, box lacrosse has always been popular north of the border. It is only in recent years that the United States has caught on to the "Canuck" brand of the sport, but only as spectators and not players. Nearly 100 percent of the players in the NLL are Canadian, and few call the United States home in the off-season. Currently in their 20th season, the NLL boasts 13

teams: the Portland LumberJax, Arizona Sting, Buffalo Bandits, Calgary Roughnecks, Colorado Mammoth, Edmonton Rush, Minnesota Swarm, Philadelphia Wings, Rochester Knighthawks, San Jose Stealth, Toronto Rock, New York Titans, and the Chicago Shamrox. They play a season beginning in late December and running through April, with play-offs and finals in May.

An interesting aspect of the indoor game is the involvement of Native American players. As might be expected of the initiators of the sport, Native Americans make up a decent percentage of the indoor lacrosse players. This is in stark contrast to the original Canadian Amateur Box Leagues, which did not allow Native American players on the pretext that they were not "professionals." Over the years and with the modern development of the game, however, more and more Native Americans are representing their heritage by playing lacrosse at the highest levels of the sport, both indoor and out.

The NLL's short field version of the game continues to grow in popularity. It has attracted a host of corporate sponsors including Reebok, Vonage, Progressive Insurance, Dodge, and Jet Blue Airways in the United States. Add Wendy's, Molson Canadian, and Yamaha to the mix from corporate Canada. This kind of sponsorship begs for attention, and the last two years has seen it on the rise both live and on television. In 2005 the NLL all-star and division final were broadcast on NBC in prime time. In 2006, ESPN stepped up to the plate to cover the finals between the Denver Mammoth and the Buffalo Bandits on live television. Interest from the business world has also been solid, spurring rapid expansion of the league over the past three years with teams added in Portland (Oregon), Edmonton (Canada), New York, and Chicago.

For hockey and lacrosse fans alike, the NLL provides hard-hitting indoor action that is both exciting and affordable. Ticket prices remain within the budget of the average fan, and the expanded television coverage will help to further the cause. Some players and enthusiasts are urging cooperative efforts between the two seeming competitors, indoor NLL and outdoor Major League Lacrosse. This new synergy may further the popularity of lacrosse and its development worldwide.

MAJOR LEAGUE LACROSSE

Major League Lacrosse (MLL) began in 2001 with the goal of showcasing the highest level of field lacrosse in the world. Founded by lacrosse enthusiasts and business professionals Jake "Body by Jake" Steinfeld, Dave Morrow, Tim Robertson, and Jim Davis. Fielding teams filled with the best players in the world, the initial teams consisted of men from some of the top academic institutions in the country. Known for years as the "intellectual's contact sport," players from prestigious schools such as Princeton, Johns Hopkins, Syracuse, Duke, Virginia, Georgetown, and Cornell filled the MLL ranks. This included some of the modern-day legends of the game: Ryan Boyle, Gary Gait, Conor Gill, Jesse Hubbard, Jay Jalbert, Mark Millon, and the superstar Powell brothers.

In just a few years the league has grown to include teams from both the East and West Coast, with the Chicago Machine, Denver Outlaws, Los Angeles Riptide, and the San Francisco Dragons representing the West. The original eastern teams are the Baltimore Bayhawks, Boston Cannons, Long Island Lizards, New Jersey Pride, Philadelphia Barrage, and Rochester Rattlers. The two conferences play a total of 60 regular season games between May and August, culminating in play-offs and the championship, all to be aired by ESPN2.

Though very much still the traditional field game of lacrosse, the MLL has added some viewer-friendly additions that truly separate the professional game from the collegiate. The first addition is a two-point goal line 15 yards from each goal that is much like the three-point land in basketball. There is a 60-second shot clock borrowed from the indoor game, and lastly a limit of three long-stick defensemen per team. Because lacrosse is such a fast sport with the ball traveling at speeds upward of 100 miles per hour, a highly visible orange ball has been chosen as the official ball of the MLL, helping both venue-based and television fans better follow the game.

At its purest, the MLL offers a version of the game that will soon become the standard for high scoring, hard hitting action, the likes of which have not been seen on sports television. With the backing of corporate sponsors such as Anheuser-Busch, New Balance, Tommy Hilfiger, and Warrior Lacrosse, and with official partnerships with Body by Jake Global, Cascade, Gatorade, Great Atlantic Lacrosse Company, Starbucks, Under Armor, and US Lacrosse, the MLL is positioned to become the next great spectator sport of our time.

COLLEGE LACROSSE

For the vast majority of lacrosse fans the number one event remains the NCAA Division 1 Championships. These are held annually in May. This is the ultimate level of play for most lacrosse players, few of whom actually go on to the pros. The Division 1 tournament is one of the most contested and coveted championships in college athletics. The 2006 final, played in Philadelphia, showcased the University of Virginia Cavaliers, capping a 17-game undefeated season by decisively beating University of Massachusetts in front of a crowd of more than 47,000 fans. In addition to

THE 2007 NCAA Men's Lacrosse Championships will be returning to Baltimore from May 26-28 at M&T Bank Stadium. Martin Schwartz, Tournament Director, expects a total sellout for the first time in the history of the event. Currently (as of May 2006) more than 13,000 tickets have been purchased. "I am urging fans to get their tickets early," Schwartz said. "The NCAA Lacrosse Championships are no longer just a series of great lacrosse games. It has become one of the nation's premier sporting events."

Today's attendance figure for the 2006 National Championship was 47,062, which broke last year's record of 44,920. The attendance today is the highest-attended NCAA Championship game this year, besting the 43,168 that saw the DI Men's Basketball Championship at the RCA Dome. Saturday's games drew nearly 50,000 fans. M&T Bank Stadium has a capacity of 70,107.

—Official Press Release from the NCAA

playing to the venue itself, ESPN broadcasted the game live on Memorial Day.

The college Division 1 Tournament begins each May, culminating a spring season that is typically 16 games long. The top 16 teams meet in an elimination tournament that lasts the entire month. Some very famous names have played in such tournaments, most notably Jim Brown, the famous NFL running back and the only person to be inducted into the College, NFL, and Lacrosse Halls of Fame.

The Division 1 Tournament is where legends are made and dynasties built, where young men play a game not for the money or promise of professional fame, but for the love of the game and school pride. Syracuse, Princeton, Maryland, and Virginia are mainstays at such tournaments; University of Massachusetts, Delaware, Georgetown, and the military academies also find invitations on a regular basis. It is the occasional dark horse, however, that adds some extra excitement to the fray, as did the University of Denver, the upstart team from the Rockies that earned a right to contend in 2006.

The NCAA's Division 2 and 3 teams also host tournaments at this time, as do all of the women's teams. This makes for a whole lot of lacrosse and a whole lot of fun for lacrosse fans nationwide. Many of the games are now broadcast on CSTV, which specializes in covering collegiate sports. After a year of controversy surrounding the powerhouse Duke men's lacrosse team, the 2006 tournament may help to put the sport of lacrosse back on track as America's newest general audience sport

CLUB LACROSSE

Scattered all over the United States and abroad are former college and high school players of every caliber who have gone "pro" in just about every area of life but the sport they love. For those of us who played in a time pre-professional lacrosse or, more realistically, just weren't that good, there were club teams. Leagues of men from 18 to 50, who love and play the sport of lacrosse, flourish all over this nation. From local indoor and outdoor leagues to local pick-up games, these leagues contain some of the sport's biggest promoters.

Though typically amateur in flavor, the club team circuit has fielded some outstanding lacrosse teams. Teams exist made up of former D-1 champions and all-Americans like the "Rusty Red," a group of former Cornell players who at 40 and older still play at the grandmaster level. From these club teams come the cream of the crop that rise to play in the World games at master and grandmaster

level. Indeed, the club system has developed the strongest sense of community within the lacrosse family. These players get together on weekends to play in local and regional tournaments, such as the Vail Shootout held annually in Vail, Colorado. This tournament hosts lacrosse teams from all over the nation and from every age group. It is the largest lacrosse tournament in the United States and is simply a hoot.

The club system also exits at the collegiate level, allowing schools that do not formally recognize lacrosse as a sport, typically in the West, to field club teams that have little school sponsorship except in name. Many of the leagues have grown increasingly competitive and have paved the way for NCAA expansion in the future. Schools like Arizona State University, University of California, Santa Barbara, University of Arizona, and San Diego have developed teams that attract high-level players from the all over the country looking to play lacrosse in the sunny West. Many of these teams now compete against their historical betters east of the Mississippi and show a level of play that is worthy of comparison with East Coast lacrosse.

HIGH SCHOOL LACROSSE

Until recently lacrosse has known little success outside of the opulent prep schools of the east coast. But now many schools both public and private have embraced the sport. Some of the most aggressive expansion has been in California, where some of the best players in the world are now being trained. San Diego, San Francisco, Los Angles, and Monterey have developed strong high school programs that produce nationally ranked players who have moved on to the Division 1 ranks. The ability for West Coast kids to play year-round is helping to catapult lacrosse into West Coast culture.

Whether boys or girls are playing, lacrosse is making a stand on the beaches of California, the deserts of Arizona, and the mountains of Colorado. Just take a look at any Division 1 roster and you will find at least one player from these states. As a matter of fact, many east coast coaches begin their summer recruitment tours in the west, visiting the summer lacrosse programs run in those state. Some even say that the next "great player" will come from the West, and come soon.

YOUTH LACROSSE

At the grass-roots level of the lacrosse craze are the many youth lacrosse programs run in communities across the country. All over the nation transplanted east coast players and "old timers" are giving back to the sport they love. Some are even making it their living, quitting the corporate world in order to help spread the game. Coach Albin Haglund is such a man. A member of the legendary 1976 undefeated Division 1 championship team from Cornell, Coach Albin has single-handedly grown the base of lacrosse in Phoenix, Arizona. His youth lacrosse league has grown to over 300 kids in just a few short years. In addition, former women's lacrosse star Jessica Livingston has developed Desert Sticks, a youth league for girls that rivals the boy's leagues in number.

Lacrosse continues to grow in these states with additions such as Elite Lacrosse, which provides the highest level of individual coaching and instruction available to Arizona youth by recruiting east coast expertise and bringing it to the west. With coaches from Division I, II, and III and assorted pro-players Elite is redefining the standard of lacrosse in the Southwest.

US LACROSSE

In the United States, US Lacrosse has led the way in the development of the sport. Prior to its founding in 1998, the lacrosse community in the United States was fragmented. The Lacrosse Foundation, US Women's Lacrosse Association, the National Junior Lacrosse Association, United States Lacrosse Coaches Association, the United States Club Lacrosse Association, and the National Lacrosse Officials Association were all brought to the negotiation table to discuss unification of human and financial resources under the auspices of US Lacrosse. This unification has paved the way for US Lacrosse to implement its mission to "provide programs and services to inspire participation while protecting the integrity of the game. We envision a future which offers people everywhere the opportunity to discover, learn, participate in, enjoy, and ultimately embrace the shared passion of the lacrosse experience" (www.uslacrosse.org).

Located in Baltimore, Maryland, US Lacrosse now acts as the governing body for lacrosse in the 50 states and United States territories. It provides unified rules and regulations for the game itself, and education and training for professionals in the lacrosse world such as coaches and officials. It also serves as a center for the research and development of upgraded safety equipment for the game, as well as a center for education and historical perspective via the Lacrosse Museum and National Hall of Fame.

EXCERPT FROM THE LACROSSE HALL OF FAME AND US LACROSSE

Considered by many to be the greatest to ever play the game of lacrosse, Jim Brown began his lacrosse career at Manhasset High School in New York where his midfield play earned him All-Star honors for three years. At Syracuse University, Brown's all-around athletic ability became evident, as he lettered in four sports and was voted the school's Athlete of the Year in 1956-57. Brown was a Second Team All-American Selection in 1956, and earned First Team Honors in 1957, finishing second in the nation in scoring his senior year. Many believe his last game was his greatest moment as a lacrosse player, as Brown scored five goals in one half of play against the nation's top players in the 1957 Collegiate North/South All-Star game. Brown went on to achieve great success with the Cleveland Browns of the National Football League, and was elected into the Pro Football Hall of Fame in 1971. Although he is best remembered for his gridiron exploits, Brown is quoted as having said, "I'd rather play lacrosse six days a week and football on the seventh."

CHAPTER 3

THE GAME OF LACROSSE AND WHERE TO LEARN IT

Lacrosse is a game of speed, skill, and physicality. The modern game reflects within it the roots of Native American warrior training. Like many contact sports, it is analogous to war. Players don armor for protection and carry a weapon in the form of a stick that they use to "attack" the goal and to "defend" it with vigorous physical play. To many observers, lacrosse seems a lawless sport, but in reality it is a sport of skill and finesse and, as the Native American roots show, a replacement for the needless violence of warfare itself. The modern game is actually one of the least injurious of team sports and lends itself to a variety of physical body types and skills. Simply put, anyone and everyone can play. Men and women, boys and girls all have a version of the sport to call their own, and the great outdoors as well as indoor tout forms of the game that allow play year round and in virtually every locale. There are also non-contact hybrids of the game such as mod-crosse and others that allow people of all ages and ability to play a less physical form of the game.

MEN'S FIELD LACROSSE

There are two versions of the men's sport: indoor, which is played in a turfed hockey rink, and outdoor, which is played on a much larger grass or turf field. The field version of the sport is becoming the most popular version of the game in the United States and internationally. It is played on a field that is 110 yards long and 60 yards wide with specific zones—offensive, defensive, and midfield—in which players must operate. Defensive players must remain on the defensive side of the field and offensive players on the offensive side. Midfield players may roam throughout the entire field. The most distinctive feature of the outdoor game is the specific equipment used by offensive and defensive players respectively, specifically, their sticks. Offensive players play with smaller sticks, while defenders may use sticks up to six feet in length. In addition, the goalies have a larger, headed stick to help in defending the net. Unlike their indoor counterparts, most field goalies wear a minimum of equipment while defending their larger six by six foot goals.

Beyond these differences in equipment is the larger strategic play of the field game. Many field games on the collegiate level are more about specific one-on-one match-ups with individual players while the pros play a more traditional game that has more fast-break opportunities. At the high school level there remains the opportunity for both fast break play as well as individual match-ups, but set offensive plays are more the norm. No matter the style of play, the field game is a rush to watch, and it is spectator and player interest that is driving the sport to new heights.

BOX LACROSSE

The indoor version of the game commonly known as box lacrosse is played predominantly in Canada

in the hockey off-season. Though dominated by Canadians, the indoor game is being played more and more in the United States. The only impediment to year-round play in some of the hotter areas such as Arizona is the oppressive summer heat that can top out at 115 degrees Fahrenheit and melt both equipment and players. The solution has been found in the many air-conditioned indoor sport facilities, in which the Canadian game is played during the hot summer days.

The game is played on a turf covered hockey rink that is 200 feet by 85 feet in size. Only five players are on the field for each team at a time and all equipment sticks are of equal length for all players except the goalie. The goalie wields a stick much like their field counterparts, but in a much different manner. The stick is typically held head down much like a hockey goalie. Other similarities to hockey is the equipment worn by the goalies, who are padded up to take powerful 100 mile an hour shots from offensive players trying to score on the four foot by four foot x 9 inch goal. The play of indoor goalies is less athletic than field goalies, and the use of the body to stop shots is prominent and in stark contrast to field goalies' tendencies to make a save using the head of the stick. The indoor game is much more contact oriented, allowing stick and body checks to players who are not even carrying the ball. This mandates a rough and tough, close quarter mode of play that rewards phenomenal stick work and quick maneuvers close to the goal in order to score a goal.

So which version of the sport is better? Fans love to debate but it is an impossible question to answer. Both versions have different skills that predominate—stickwork for indoors, and dodging and athleticism in the field game. Indeed, the participation and cultivation of both versions add to making a "complete" player in the sport. As this book strives to cover the best of both games, so should a player strive to play both versions of the game in order to become a great player. Lacrosse history is rife with examples of indoor players excelling in the field game, such as Gary and Paul Gait, while field players have begun to make their mark in the indoor arenas, such as Josh Sims and the Powells.

WOMEN'S LACROSSE

In addition to the men's versions of the game, the women's sport of lacrosse has been played internationally for years. The women's game is played on a 110 by 60 yard field with specific zones for offensive play delineated in front of each goal. As the women's version of the sport does not allow for much stick or body contact, less equipment is worn and superior stick skill and ball movement must carry the day. In fact, the women's sticks do not maintain a deep mesh pocket, as do the men's, so keeping the ball in the stick while dodging and cutting is a testament to women's technical skills with the stick. Many a men's team have challenged their female counterparts to a friendly scrimmage using women's sticks, only to be humiliated with their inability to catch, throw, and cradle.

POSITIONS

Players in both field and indoor lacrosse play specific positions depending on their individual abilities and proclivities. The indoor game maintains offensive players called runners, defenders, and a goalkeeper. The field version has four basic positions: attack, midfield, defense, and goalie. Each position has specific duties on the playing field. In the indoor version of the game, offensive and defensive players substitute through the box, hockey style. In the field game there is a substitution area in which players also change. In both venues there is a specific number of players per team side—a total of six, five plus the goalie, in the indoor game, and 10 on the field. However, in the field version of the game a certain number of players must always remain on the offensive and the defensive sides of the field. Three attackmen must always be present on the offensive side, and three defensemen on the defensive side. Midfielders may roam the full field and play a mix of both offense and defense.

Attack

The attackman's responsibility is essentially to drive the offense by scoring goals. They are restricted to the offensive end of the field and only play defense while attempting to stop the defensive squad of the opposing team from "clearing" the ball out of the defensive zone. A good attackman has excellent stick work with both hands and possesses excellent athletic maneuvering in order to attack the goal from any direction. The attackmen are among the most skilled players on the field and should ideally represent the backbone of any team offense. Scoring goals is their number one job.

Midfield

The midfielders are the workhorses of lacrosse, playing both offense and defense over the entire length of the field. They are also a key to the transition game, moving the ball from the defensive to offensive sides of the field. A good midfielder possesses solid stick work and incredible levels of fitness. They must also have a solid grasp of the entire flow of the game as well as the ability to play both offense and defense. On each midfield "line" there is typically one player whose specialty is the face-off. The face-off specialist is a powerful athlete with lightening-fast reflexes. It is his job to get possession of the ball and prevent the other team doing so. Some levels of the game recruit face-off men who do nothing else. They do the face-off,

and then sprint off the field to rest until they are called to the center again. Each team should have three midfielders on the field at a time and possess three or more complete midfield lines to be rotated in and out of play during a game.

Defense

The defenseman is the protector of the goalie and is predominantly responsible for defending the goal by utilizing a combination of skills including physical play, solid stick work, and hard checking. In addition they must have the skill to move the ball from the defensive to offensive zones of the field after taking the ball away from an offensive player or after the goalie makes a save. This is called a "clear" and is an important aspect of defensive play. The defenseman generally restricts his play to the defensive end of the field. A good defenseman should be able to react quickly in game situations. Agility and aggressiveness are necessary as is understanding of offensive players' methods, to better stop them from scoring. In the past, great stick work was not a necessity, but as the sport grows, the agile and stick-savvy defenseman is becoming a standard. In the indoor game, defensemen play with the same length stick as offensive players, while field d-sticks vary in length from 52 to 72 inches in length. Each team should have three defensemen on the field of play, but may substitute a long stick defenseman into a midfield line, a long stick middie, if additional defense is needed.

Goalie

The quarterback of the defensive team and the heart of the entire squad is the goalie. It is the goalkeeper's responsibility to protect the goal and stop the opposing team from scoring. They are the last line of defense and the first to touch the ball on offensive when a stop is made. Goalies come in

© William Klos

all shapes and sizes and are often the best player on the field, possessing a higher understanding of the game. The goalie leads the defense by reading the situation and directing the defensemen to react. Great goalies should have excellent hand/eye coordination, leadership skills, unflinching reaction to the ball, and a strong and commanding voice. Goalies need to be strong mentally because so much pressure is placed on them during a game. Each team has one goalie in the goal during play, and once you have experienced players taking 100 mile an hour shots at you from every conceivable angle, you will understand that goalies are indeed unique (read: crazy) individuals.

WHERE TO LEARN LACROSSE

Lacrosse camps are the obvious place. All throughout the off-season, the world's best players and coaches can be found manning hundreds of instructional camps held throughout the country. Warrior, Nike, Brine, STX, and many other manufacturers, sponsor companies, and individual players organize these camps to help further the game of lacrosse by offering up close and personal training and coaching from the best in the game. From junior level to the pre-collegiate, thousands of kids from all over the country attend these camps that typically are held on the campuses of East Coast lacrosse powerhouse teams. Imagine being a first year player getting personal attention from Casey Powell, Gary Gait, or coach Jamie Munro, while having the opportunity to play up to 20 "mini-games" a session. Indeed, the summer camp system acts as a de facto training and recruiting ground for future talent. It is a way for players to get in front of coaches that may determine their futures and for younger players to get experience at a level beyond what is typically available to them. From California to Canada the lacrosse camp experience is a must for anyone serious about the game. It is a way to learn, play, and get seen, and to develop the kind of lifelong friendships that lacrosse seems to promote best.

Many people begin to learn lacrosse from print, Internet, television, and other media. As the message of lacrosse continues to spread, it has spawned a multi-media presence that cannot be ignored. Internet sites, magazines, blogs, and more are allowing interested parties to find out more and more about his amazing sport. So hot has the topic been that *Sports Illustrated,* the icon of sports news, published a historic nine page article entitled "Get on the Stick," telling of the meteoric rise in popularity of lacrosse on television and radio. A simple Google search for "lacrosse" yields over a million sites for information, equipment, and more. ESPN and CSTV have committed prime time spots to coverage of games, and magazines like *Inside Lacrosse* and *Lacrosse Magazine* are increasing in distribution. Even the unsettling news concerning the Duke lacrosse team has sparked thousands upon thousands of searches for information on the game and beyond.

Indeed, getting additional media to help to spread the popularity of the game is paramount to its success. As with many new trends, the Internet is filled with all forms of lacrosse websites to fan the fire. Sites that offer training, team information, coaching tips, equipment, and advice fill the computer realm, giving the increasingly computer savvy generation of youngsters access to a plethora of information on the sport they love. It has gone so far as to spawn a slew of strategic relationships with additional web and cable based networks such as Lacrosse TV, which provides broadcasts of all NLL games via cable as well as computer interactivity. The magazines, websites, and broadcasts combine to make a formidable information-based marketing and public relations machine that is directly affecting the consumer players of today. Lacrosse is now being mentioned regularly in the popular culture. Television and radio personalities such as Howard Stern have complimented the skill and physicality of the game. There is even a lacrosse video game for Playstation that is being revamped with updated graphics and technology, to be re-released in the near future. North, South, East, or West, lacrosse is soon to be a household name.

DEVELOPING THE COMPLETE PLAYER

A large portion of this book is dedicated to two of the three parts necessary for becoming a complete player. First is basic athletic ability, which is covered in Part 1 of this book and covers a variety of areas: strength training, agility training, flexibility, and conditioning. The second part of becoming a complete player is skills development: cradling, throwing, catching, shooting, dodging, and ground balls. The third aspect of the complete player is field sense and an understanding of the game including: field positioning, off-ball play, flow, transition and fast breaks, discipline, and attitude. This last portion of the complete player is purposefully left open to personal interpretation and for the individual player, coaches, and parents to foster. This book is focused on the first two aspects of a complete player and offers a glimpse into the conceptual and pragmatic applications of the third. For now, we will provide a solid physical basis for the complete player trilogy. Good luck and train hard!

PART II

···

Good Nutrition, the Right Equipment, and Proper Conditioning

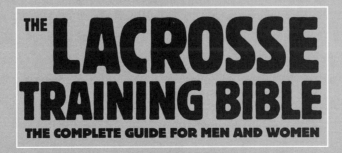

CHAPTER 4

FUEL

Part of becoming a great lacrosse player is becoming a complete athlete. By this we mean that a player wishing to excel in the sport must approach everything that they do holistically. Skills, conditioning, agility, and strength are physical characteristics of an athlete that cannot be optimized if we ignore certain facts concerning the limitations of physical training. We cannot create an athlete with our efforts in the gym or on the field alone. Proper nutrition and hydration are keys to developing the abilities we strive for. Many high school lacrosse players ignore these aspects of their training, though it is during their formative years that good habits and a working understanding of how nutritional factors go hand in hand with physical training are critical. This section of the book will explain what you need to know about nutrition. The old adage is true—you are what you eat.

Nutritional studies should begin with an understanding of the vital roles played by food in the recovery and fueling systems of the body. The former is essential for recuperation from play and for achieving goals that begin in the weight room and at the track. The latter directly affects the quality of play and off-field activities by literally fueling the body for optimal performance. Like a formula racecar, the oil and gas we place in the machine will equal performance on the track.

First one must understand the basics of food itself and how it affects performance. Fats, carbohydrates, and protein are the components of food itself. Often called macronutrients, these are the nutrients recognized by the body.

CARBOHYDRATES

Carbohydrates are the fuel for any and all physical activities. Most athletes should strive to obtain approximately 50 percent of all their calories from carbs. When consumed, carbohydrates are broken down by the body into a usable energy source called glycogen. Glycogen is then stored in the liver and in the muscles themselves. This allows the body to access glycogen for fuel as needed. The ability for the body to store this energy source is limited, and thus an athlete is forced to refuel these reserves daily. The storage and use of glycogen is muscle-specific. If you perform a heavy leg workout and deplete the source of energy within that muscle, it cannot tap glycogen from other areas of the body and therefore fatigues. That is why proper fueling is so important to the athlete.

Eating carbohydrates daily is the only way to replenish our glycogen stores. But not all carbohydrates are created equal. There are complex carbs and simple carbs, both of which provide energy. Simple carbs, however, have a faster burn time than complex carbs. It is like adding a piece of paper to a fire. It will ignite and burn quickly, as do simple carbs. Complex carbs are like putting a log on a fire. It takes longer to burn and thus gives off energy slowly and over time.

A simple or complex carbohydrate is rated primarily by its position on the glycemic index. When choosing which carbohydrates to eat, you should make an effort to consume those with a lower glycemic index. These carbohydrates typically are high in fiber and absorb more slowly into the blood stream. This provides for a more sustained source of glycogen for activity. As an athlete it is best to avoid high glycemic foods and replace them with lower glycemic choices. The chart at the back of this book will help you to make better choices in your fuel foods. Be sure to maintain a level of carbohydrate consumption that will provide both adequate calories and a better access to glycogen for the body. Limit your intake of high-glycemic foods to 10 percent of your total carbs consumed.

PROTEIN

Protein is the building block nutrient of the body. It allows us to build muscle and repair any damage occurring as a result of intense training. Athletes should consume a diet of at least 20-30 percent high-quality protein per day. As with carbohydrates, protein is also made up of smaller chemical building blocks that the body uses. These building blocks are called amino acids. It is the amino acids in protein that give the body its utility. The best food for obtaining amino acids is a lean meat protein such as steak, chicken, or fish. If consuming meat is not an option for you, that is not a problem because protein also comes from eggs and some milk-based products such as whey. The best protein powders and protein supplements are made from whey. It is important to eat enough protein every day without overeating. Excess protein, no matter from what source, is converted to and stored as fat, with unwanted weight gain.

Protein is more difficult to digest and break down than other nutrients, so it is important to distribute your protein intake throughout the day. Your body is only able to digest and absorb about 30-35 grams of protein at any one meal (or approximately every 3 hours). Do not try to consume massive amounts all at once.

Even though protein is predominantly a building block nutrient, the body can use it as fuel. Any aerobic activity that lasts for 45 minutes continuously, such as long distance running, will use protein as a fuel source to some extent. Using protein as fuel is a fast way to beak down lean body mass. It is not a goal of a lacrosse athlete to take off what you worked so hard to put on. By consuming a consistent intake of high quality proteins we can insure proper recovery of muscle tissue and further development of musculature, the number one goal of any strength and conditioning program.

FAT

Fat, though vilified by the many, is essential to your body's ability to function. Fat acts as long-term storage of excess calories, assists the immune system, and protects joints and organs. It also stores the essential vitamins A, D, E, and K. Because of its nature, fat is very high in calories per volume, and thus its intake should be limited. Optimal intake for athletes should be no more than 25-35 percent of calories coming from fat. As with protein and carbs, not all fat is created equal. There are three types of fat: saturated fats that derive mainly from animal sources such as meat and butter, monosaturated fats such as olive oil and fish oil, and polyunsaturated fats such as soybean oil. An athlete's consumption of fat should come from unsaturated sources, usually found in plants, and from monosaturated fats. Fat is the primary energy source for endurance athletes, and though it does not have an effect on blood sugar levels, it does tend to slow absorption of carbohydrates. So although it is important to have fats in our diet for good health and recovery, over consumption of fat will lead to poor athletic performance.

HOW MUCH TO EAT

Now that we have reviewed the kinds of nutrients your body needs, the next question is how much of each kind? The number of calories a person needs is determined by many factors: genetics, gender, age, body composition, activity levels, and so on. Athletes especially need to make sure that they are getting all the fuel and nutrients their body needs.

Though there is not a hard and fast method for determining exactly how much food to eat, there are some rules of thumb or guidelines for athletes. To estimate your required protein intake, take your body weight in pounds and multiply it by 0.9.

Body weight (lbs) x 0.9 = grams of protein needed daily

To estimate your required carbohydrate intake, take your weight and multiply by 2.5.

Body weight (lbs) x 2.5 = grams of carbohydrates needed daily

To estimate your required fat intake, multiply body weight by .025.

Body weight (lbs) x .025 = grams of fat per day

Next, to compute the total caloric content of your daily food intake, add together:

Protein intake total x 4 calories = total calories

Carbohydrates intake total x 4 calories = total calories

Fat intake total x 9 calories = total calories

Add the last three values together to get a total caloric intake per day. For example, if you are a typical 200-pound athlete, your numbers might look like this:

Daily protein = 180 grams/day x 4 calories = 720 calories from protein/day

Daily carbohydrates = 500 grams/day x 4 = 2,000 calories from carbohydrates/day

Daily fat = 50 grams/day x 9 = 450 calories from fat/day

Total calories/day = 3,170 calories/day

These numbers can give you an approximate base line for proper fueling and nutrition, but one based, please note, only on your scale weight. It does not take into consideration your body composition, which means how much of your body weight is lean body mass and not fat. What is being calculated is the total number of calories needed to maintain current body and muscle mass, barring any need to decrease body fat or to increase lean body mass. Nevertheless, this base-line number gives you a reference point from which to start estimating the calories you need for maximum performance.

How To Eat

Now that you have determined how much food you need, it is important to know when to eat and how that will maximize your results in training. Eating three large meals a day has been an American staple for years. Unfortunately this pattern is not ideal for athletes because it allows for too large a fluctuation of blood sugar levels. Eating only three times a day allows blood sugar levels to drop quite low between meals. These drops mean there is not a constant level of blood sugar and this energy available to our muscles. Eating five smaller meals a day is a much better plan for keeping blood sugar and energy levels at maximum. To figure out what a typical meal should look like nutritionally on this system, take your breakdown of what you should eat and apply these formulas:

Amount of protein/day = 'x' grams divided by 5 daily meals = protein grams per meal

Amount of carbohydrates = 'x' grams divided by 5 meals = carbohydrate grams per meal

Amount of fat = 'x' grams divided by 5 meals = fat grams per meal

For example, if we take the 200-pound athlete assumed in our previous calculations and apply these formulas, we get these numbers: 180 grams of protein/day divided by 5 meals = 36 grams of protein/meal, 500 grams of carbohydrates/day divided by 5 meals = 100 grams of carbohydrates/meal, and 50 grams of fat/day divided by 5 meals = 10 grams of fat/meal.

That breaks down what you need into five balanced and complete meals per day. For optimal digestion of these many meals, especially protein absorption, eat every three hours throughout the day. Here is an example of a simple diet designed to increase strength and lean muscle while decreasing body fat.

For some athletes, eating on this regular schedule and eating this much is a daunting task. Do your best. The right diet is very important if you want to get maximum performance out of the body machine. Fortunately, there are many meal replacement bars, shakes, and even some relatively healthy fast food alternatives (such as grilled chicken sandwich without mayo). You can eat properly on the run. However, all of this may be done in by poor food choices.

Eating quality sources of protein, fats, and carbs is very important to athletic performance and overall health. Be sure to choose fresh fruits and vegetables, lean cuts of meat, and good sources of

---

Sample Diet

7AM Breakfast:
1-2 servings of fruits, yogurt, or vegetables
1-2 serving of All-Bran or oatmeal
4-6 egg whites (scrambled or hard boiled)

10AM Post Training:
1 Recovery Shake or
2 servings of fruits, yogurt, or vegetables
1 can of tuna (water packed)

1PM Lunch:
1 serving of yogurt or vegetables
1 cup brown rice
1 chicken breast or can of tuna
1 piece of fruit

4PM Snack:
1 serving of yogurt or vegetables
1 can tuna

7PM Dinner:
1 serving of vegetables
1 piece fish, chicken, or lean steak
1 piece of fruit

fat. Avoid fast food completely and keep processed foods to a minimum. Become a reader of labels and avoid ingredients such as high fructose corn syrup and any hydrogenated or partially hydrogenated oils. Also do your best to limit your intake of processed foods. A good rule of thumb is that if it does not have an expiration date, don't eat it.

Read the labels, paying close attention to serving size, and apply the previous formulas to determine the calories allowed by your meal plan. Combined with your training program, good nutrition will yield incredible results.

Pre-Training or Game Eating

What and when to eat on a daily basis is vital to your health and fitness, but your pre-practice/game/workout nutrition can make or break your performance. Prior to training or game time, it important to both prefuel and prehydrate your body. The following are some recommendations for preperformance and recovery nutrition:

1. Drink 16-20 ounces (2-3 glasses) of water 20-30 minutes before the activity. Avoid drinking any beverage that is high in sugar or in protein because they impede the ability of the small intestine to absorb water efficiently and therefore may help to dehydrate you.

2. Two to three hours before a practice/game/workout eat a meal that is high in complex carbohydrates, low protein, and very low fat. This will provide energy for the event without taxing the body to digest hard to absorb protein or nutrients.

3. During the activity continue to drink water or use an electrolyte replacement drink mixed with water. Keep drinking throughout the entire activity.

4. 20-30 minutes after practice/game/workout

eat some form of carbohydrate to replenish your lost glycogen reserves. Recent studies have found carbohydrate uptake into the muscle is at least twice as efficient right after exercise. They have also found that fructose (sugar from fruits) is a much better way to do this because, unlike other sugars (carbohydrates), it goes from your blood directly into your muscle, not first to the liver like the rest of the carbohydrates. So enjoy fruit following your exercise, and you'll be putting twice as much carbohydrate right back into your tank!

5. Within 90 minutes of this post-workout snack eat 30-50 grams of protein so that your body is ready to begin repairing itself. This is when a high quality protein shake should be used.

Proper fueling before, during, and after the activity is the key to your actual performance on the field or in the gym that day. But of course it is only part of the equation. Your regular, seven-days-a-week nutrition plan is really where the rubber meets the road when it comes to overall performance. If you do not have and follow faithfully a regular nutrition plan, your performance will lag your potential.

Always start your day with a healthy breakfast. Breakfast is the most important meal of the day. This is because, after sleeping all night long without eating (fasting), the glycogen in your liver is nearly depleted. Eating a healthy meal in the morning will help your body to prime itself for the tasks of the day. Not eating a good breakfast may lead to your body taking protein and glycogen from your muscles to maintain blood sugar levels. This can also effect brain function and hormone production in a way that will impede proper function, which is why schools are pushing proper morning nutrition for all students. This is particularly difficult for high school athletes who rarely eat a good breakfast and who do not have access to healthy snacks during the day.

Note that the above recipe can be augmented depending on the athletes goals in body mass makeup. For an athlete wishing to increase body mass, additional calories may be added by substituting whole milk. If an athlete is trying to drop weight, then dropping the juice component may help. No matter the goal, a simple electrolyte/protein shake post-training is now a staple in professional athletic training and should be come a staple in your training as well.

HYDRATION

The body can actually survive without food for quite some time, but deny it water and we die quickly. The human body is made up predominantly of water (70 percent), and keeping it hydrated is a simple way to keep healthy. For athletes, it is a must. Losing precious water, together with salt and electrolytes, is unavoidable as we sweat. Replenishing those substances is imperative. Waiting to feel thirsty before drinking is a no-no. You must continually hydrate to maintain performance levels. Thus, while participating in any of these training sessions, drink 8-10 glasses of water each day at minimum. This will insure you replace the fluids lost during exercise.

Keep drinking water continuously throughout the day. You may also choose to consume any of the popular sports drinks while exercising. These drinks provide electrolytes, salts, and simple carbs to speed in recovery and help performance. Drink water throughout the day and sport drinks while training. A simple self-test to see if you are properly hydrated is a urine examination. If your urine

AFTER intense exercise it is important to replenish glycogen levels as well as provide your body with muscle-repairing protein. Timing is key since intense exercise creates an anabolic (tissue-building) environment in the body by stimulating the release of growth hormone and testosterone. After training, with these hormones at a heightened state, your body is primed for tissue growth and repair. This is also the time when your muscles and tissues will most rapidly replace the nutrients used during exercise. Ideally, within 30 minutes of training/game/practice a small meal or snack meal replacement beverage or bar should be consumed to maximize recovery results. This post-training snack should contain some simple carbohydrates in the form of fruit, electrolyte powder, and approximately 30 grams of protein. After consuming this drink, rest and recovery begins, culminating in the consumption of a healthy, well-balanced meal about 90 minutes later. Here is a recipe for post-training recovery drinks:

SHAKE #1—RECOVERY SHAKE RECIPE

2 scoops of quality protein powder
1 scoop of electrolyte powder
1 banana
1 cup nonfat milk or orange juice
One serving contains approximately 450
   calories, 90 g carbohydrate, 30 g
      protein, and 4 g fat.

is light yellow or clear, you are well-hydrated. If your urine is yellow or dark yellow, then you need to hydrate more.

NUTRITIONAL SUPPLEMENTS

Many fitness professionals, physicians, and layman alike have fallen victim to the nutritional supplement craze. Multivitamins, minerals, powders, and the like fill the shelves of our stores, driven by a never-ending marketing barrage from manufacturers. Millions of dollars are spent each year by athletes in the pursuit of an "edge" in their performance. Most of this money is completely wasted on sub-par products that have minimal effect beyond a placebo. It is a sad fact that the majority of nutritional supplements simply do not work. The reason is that your body is not particularly responsive to artificial nutrients. Indeed, the result of much oversupplementation is a syndrome called nutritional fatigue, caused by the body's inability to process manufactured nutrients. So how does an athlete, in the pursuit of higher achievement, get all the effective nutritional support that he needs? The answer is in properly fueling the body using good nutrition derived from high-quality, natural foods.

Eating high-quality calories and nutrients is very important to the performance of an athlete. The nutritional guidelines we gave explained the food needed in terms of the macronutrients. Carbs remain a vital source for recovery and performance. You must continually fuel your body with foods that are as close to the natural source as possible. In the case of necessary vitamins and minerals, a wide variety of raw whole foods such as fruits and vegetables provide natural sources.

It is best to look at fruits and vegetables as your source for vitamins, while carbs, proteins, and fat act as both your building blocks and fuel sources. Though it may be more convenient to pop a multivitamin each day, it is better by far to increase your intake of whole raw fruits and vegetables to insure proper absorption of the nutrients you seek. One caveat, however, concerns the preparation of your foods. Overcooking any food destroys many of the enzymes necessary for its proper digestion. In addition, overcooking can also leach food of its vitamin and mineral content.

Eating uncooked fruits and vegetables is the best way to obtain the full benefits that the food has to offer.

The challenge to eating right is typically one of convenience. Going to the market to get raw foods is often difficult in our busy day-to-day lives. It seems much more time efficient and cost effective to rely on supplements from a bottle or a jar. The effort to get good protein, however, will repay you in both general health and performance. This is why team chefs have appeared on the roster of many professional teams. Though not something most teams can afford, it testifies to how important eating properly is regarded by the pros.

Whether you have time to eat good wholesome foods or not, it is still important to optimize your performance. And though we would prefer you to eat fresh foods in their stead, there are some beneficial supplements that we recommend.

1. **Glutamine.** Glutamine is a supplement that can be found in dairy products and whey protein. It is an amino acid that has been reported to increase cell hydration and optimal intake is 4–10 grams of glutamine following exercise to replenish depleted glutamine pools.

2. **Vitamin C.** Vitamin C in the form of citrus fruits and juices, fresh berries, and green leafy vegetables is best. Vitamin C is a natural antioxidant vitamin that may help in the repair and maintenance of collagen tissue and may enhance immune function. Since intense exercise may suppress immune function, postexercise may be the best time to supplement with 500 mg of vitamin C.

3. **Vitamin E.** Vitamin E can be consumed in the form of vegetable oils, nuts, seeds, and raw wheat germ; this antioxidant vitamin

may relieve some of the oxidative tissue damage responsible for delayed-onset muscle soreness from heavy training. Having a regular intake of 100-400 mg/day may be of benefit.

4. **Zinc**. Zinc comes from animal protein (especially dark meat), oysters, mushrooms, whole grains, and Brewer's yeast and is an important constituent of hundreds of enzymes involved in digestion and immune function. Since zinc levels drop for several hours post-exercise, the basic dose is 25 mg/day.

5. **Electrolytes**. Electrolyte replacement drinks in liquid and powder form help to replenish salts, minerals, and water lost during intense training. These products help an athlete to quickly replenish those essential nutrients while hydrating and fueling, with simple carbs, your energy reserves. Drinks such as this should be used during intense activity and may be used just after training or play as part of your recovery. This helps to replenish the body during the critical post-exercise window in which the body craves to have its tank topped off. There are many options to choose from in this genre of supplements, the most popular being the ubiquitous Gatorade. Just be sure to use these products for what they were designed for—supplementing and recovery, not smooth drinking pleasure. Overuse of such items may actually have negative effects on the body. Though marketed often as a "soft drink," these are indeed supplements, and their use should be approached as such and not taken lightly.

6. **Protein**. As previously described, protein intake is paramount for optimal performance in an athlete's recovery from high intensity training or play. The ability to eat the amount of protein prescribed to most athletes is a culinary challenge. A 6-ounce can of tuna typically provides around 30 grams of protein for consumption. A 200-pound athlete using the formula provided in this book would need a daily intake of 180 grams of protein, or six cans of tuna each day! This can be problematic for many to say the least, so supplementing with a good quality protein powder can help. Soy, egg, or whey protein supplements are readily available at any health food store. The key issue is to make sure that the protein contained therein provides all of the essential amino acids, compounds that make up protein. Due to the processing of some protein sources using heat, much of the amino acid profile and cofactors such as the enzymes needed to properly assimilate them are damaged. Read the labels carefully and understand that a rare, lean steak is still a better option than any protein supplement on the market.

PERFORMANCE ENHANCEMENT DRUGS

In the pursuit of ever bigger, stronger, faster athletes there is a temptation to fast track performance and training via the use of performance enhancement drugs, namely anabolic steroids, human growth hormone, and stimulants. The unfortunate reality of these drugs is that they do indeed work to increase recovery time and performance, but at a terrible cost. The use of these substances is indeed tempting, and the access to these items is widespread even at the high-school level. It is important to keep this in mind while preparing lacrosse players for a future in the game. The benefits that can possibly be gained by science and chemistry are detrimental to one's long-term health. Patience, hard work, and a positive mental attitude will carry any dedicated athlete to the top without the use of such dangerous substances.

There is an unfortunate reality that we must also discuss: the use of common items considered "okay," by many coaches, players, and parents, but remain by definition performance enhancers, such as caffeine, anti-inflammatories, and bronchodilators. All of the aforementioned are readily and legally available to a player in the form of coffee or other "energy" drinks, or ephedrine-based products. None of these substances should be used without proper supervision of a physician. All of these items can be obtained readily from a convenience store or pharmacy and seem to many quite innocuous, yet all are listed by most athletic commissions as performance enhancers. Player, coach, and parent alike must address the use of these grey area products, and their use should be strongly discouraged.

© Alex Kerney

CHAPTER FIVE

THE RIGHT EQUIPMENT

Many of us start playing lacrosse as kids with a mix of borrowed equipment and hand-me-downs: a battered helmet and old glove that sort of fit us, a stick that looked like it had seen combat on D-Day, and pads that barely stayed on. After a few hours on the field we did not have to be told about the advantages of having the right equipment. The right equipment—stick, helmet, glove, and pads—is not just useful, it is essential to playing the game well. Let's talk about what you need to know to make good choices in equipping yourself to play lacrosse.

There are some well-known brands of lacrosse gear—Warrior, Harrow, STX, Gait/DeBeer, and Brine—as well as some new boutique and specialized brands developing in the market place. These smaller manufactures include Mohawk, Talon, Shock Doctor, Riddell, Shamrock, and Maverick to name a few. All of the manufactures, both small and large, provide a wide array of high-quality equipment for each individual player's needs. Go online and read the reviews. Or better yet, grab some friends and try out their gear to see if it works for you. A basic set up for boys lacrosse can run from $150- $500 depending on the level of equipment you choose. Regardless of your entry point, modern manufacturing provides the best lacrosse gear ever created for safety, efficacy, and fun.

THE STICK

Arguably the most important piece of individual equipment, the lacrosse stick, also known as the "crosse," has three basic parts. The top of the stick is called the head. Inside the head is the mesh, a basket-like material where the ball sits. Below that extends the shaft, and finally, at the opposite end, the butt-end of the stick. Modern heads are made of plastic, though one may still find traditionally made Native American heads handcrafted out of wood and natural fibers. These sticks are more and more utilized as objects d'art or for decoration in Native American rituals. Fewer players use them, though some women's teams still do.

There are various head designs from the different major manufacturers. Names you should look at and consider include Warrior, STX, Brine, Harrow, DeBeer/Gait, and some smaller productions houses such as Shamrock and Mohawk International Lacrosse. The variation in design is staggering, though the basic triangular design is universal. Differences in sidewall and scoop, stiffness and pinch are the specifics that separate the designs. These differences will be obvious to you when you have the stick in hand.

THE MESH

Situated in the head of all lacrosse sticks is the mesh. The mesh is the net-like device that holds the ball while in play. Mesh technology has given us various designs as well as many materials, though nylon twine now prevails. The most distinctive mesh type is the traditional leather stringing popular

BRINE's Truth stick for men has full Offset® for maximum control and feel, and has a narrow face to increase ball retention and accuracy.

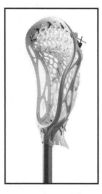  

BRINE's Clutch stick for men has the same full Offset® and narrow face as the Truth, but adds multiple sidewall holes for custom stringing.

BRINE's top women's stick, the Epic, has top rail height/scoop corners raised to increase whip and allow for a natural pocket location. It includes bottom rail drops at the ball stop for increased pocket depth and additional stringing holes for customizable stringing.

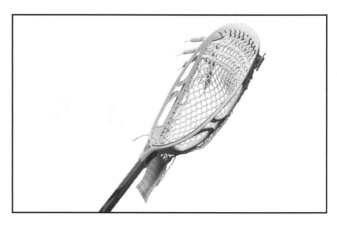

The Eraser™, BRINE's women's goalie stick, has an open sidewall for reduced weight.

with "old school" players. This mesh gives the most feel to the ball and the best support while shooting. The major drawback is the upkeep. Because the mesh itself is woven by hand, it is as variable as the leather that supports it. Natural fibers change with the weather and must be painstakingly maintained. Once it is "perfect," a traditional pocket can't be beat. The variations of traditional pockets run the gamut from traditional regular or traditional tight weave to pita-pocket, rock-it-pocket, and the doucher.

Most popular these days are the synthetic pre-woven meshes. There are a few different types of this mesh. Soft mesh is often used by beginning players because its pliable nature allows for effortless catching. Ten-diamond hard mesh is the most popular of the hard meshes, though the larger six-diamond mesh combines the feel of traditional mesh with the ease of maintaining a hard mesh. There is the four-holed monster mesh. The greatest benefit of this type of mesh is ease of maintenance. With no adjustments, other than to throwing strings, and no natural fibers to maintain with oils or seals, they are essentially maintenance-free. The fun benefits of such industrial fibers is their variation in mesh size as well as colors. Today you can get mesh kits in a rainbow of colors including day-go and neon.

Though the mesh itself is becoming more and more standard, each individual pocket is different. How you choose to string your pocket gets to the true art of stick stringing. Some players like the pocket high in the head, others prefer to center it, and still others want it at the bottom. The site and the depth of the pocket are also personal choices, as are the methods and number of shooting strings in the head (see photos). Depending on the position you play, some pockets are preferred. In the American field game, attackmen often like their pockets at the bottom, so the can keep control while driving one-on-one. This type of pocket also has a quick release point for feeding. These are all personal decisions. As long as a head stays within the dimensions specified by the official rules, it is legal for play.

THE SHAFT AND BUTT

The shaft of a lacrosse stick varies greatly in composition. Materials from old-fashioned wood to titanium and Kevlar are used to make light, heavy, octagonal, rounded, and even triangular shafts. Most older players enjoy the heavier shafts that simulate the wooden shafts used until the 1980s, while most newer players tend toward the high-tech lightweight shafts, which are hundreds of times more durable than natural materials. The latest trend in shaft design uses carbon fiber and composite shafts and some do not bend. Others are designed to keep their flexibility. They often come with a rubberized skin that gives a superb grip.

The last part of the stick is the butt-end. Regulations specify that it is to be covered at all times. This small part of the stick is actually quite important because a less than adequate butt-end can ruin a perfect pass or shot by allowing the bottom hand to slip off the stick. Whether made as a solid plug or covered with yards of tape or rubber or plastic, the butt-end is another area for personalized attention.

The cost of modern lacrosse sticks run from $30 for a basic head with an aluminum shaft to over $300 for the ultralightweight head with a high-tech shaft. Whatever your budget and choice, the final measure of a player will be found in his ability to use the stick, not in its construction.

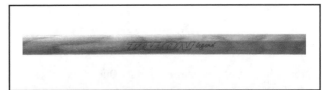

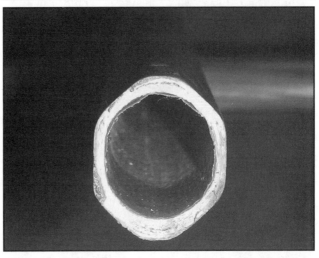

(top) A close-up, side view of the Talon Legend™ shaft. This shaft combines the warmth and aesthetic appeal of traditional wood with the strength and lightweight performance of today's high-tech materials. It is handmade through a proprietary process of layering ash wood veneer over a high tech composite core.
(bottom) An end view of the Talon Legend™ shaft, showing its hollow core.

(top) A right-side view of the Talon Grip™ end cap. This end cap is designed to replicate an eagle's talons clutching a lacrosse ball, and is a contemporary reproduction of the end of an Ojibwe ceremonial war club. The long sleeve on the end cap fits tight on the shaft, thereby replacing the need to use tape to secure the end cap from slipping.
(bottom left) A left-side view of the Talon Grip™ end cap.
(bottom right) A bottom view of the Talon Grip™ end cap

All photos pictured on this page (page 33) © Talon Lacrosse, LLC, 2007

33

As determined by the US Lacrosse Rules and Regulations, a lacrosse stick must conform to certain standard dimensions. Offensive sticks must be between 40-42 inches in length if used by attackmen and midfielders. Defensemen must use a stick 52-72 inches long. The head of the stick can be made of wood or plastic and must be 6.5-10 inches wide, except a goalie's, which may be 10-12 inches wide. Within the head of the stick there must be a mesh pocket. Placing a ball in the mesh and holding the stick horizontally determines the maximum depth for a legal pocket. The top of the ball must not go below the bottom edge of the sidewall.

These specifications apply only to the field player. In the indoor version of the sport, sticks are all uniform lengths of 42 inches. The size of the heads and the pocket depth are not regulated. Many a box player will customize their heads by "baking" or heating them in some manner until the plastic becomes malleable. They then "pinch" the bottom sidewalls together so that it becomes almost impossible to check a ball out of the stick. In addition, indoor players have no pocket depth limit, so it is not uncommon to find a player with a pocket big enough to hold many a ball.

THE BALL

An official lacrosse ball must conform to the specifications published by lacrosse's organizing body, US Lacrosse. The rules state, "the ball must be made of solid rubber and can be white, yellow, or orange. The ball is 7.75-8 inches in circumference and 5-5.25 ounces." The size and weight of a ball are thus standardized, as are the permitted colors. In addition to the official sanctioned white, orange, and yellow, one can also find red, blue, neon green, glow-in-the-dark, and even tie-dyed balls.

A lacrosse ball has some specific features that should not be overlooked. First is its surface. A new ball is somewhat "grippy" due to its rubberized texture. As it is used, this surface becomes "polished" and slippery. Such balls should not be used in practice or play because they will slip around in your pocket and make you throw inconsistently. Balls are also hard enough to cause serious damage if you are struck with one. It is advisable to always wear both gloves and helmets while throwing around. A second option is "sponge balls" that are the same size as game balls but not the same weight. These soft balls are recommended for youth and novice players. In a pinch, even tennis balls can be used.

THE GLOVE

The second most important piece of personal equipment is your glove. Choose your gloves carefully because they will determine how well you are able to handle your stick and thus play the game. Protective gloves today are made of high-tech materials that are lightweight, durable, and highly protective. In sizes and shapes to fit any size player, today's gloves are a marvel of protective engineering. From a simple nylon pair at $40 to Kevlar reinforced, fully articulated supergloves that can run $200, the protection offered is unparalleled. Serious players always practice with their gloves on to maintain their abilities on the field. Though the rules prohibit it, some "old school" players and club players alter their gloves by cutting out the palms. This is a holdover from the days when gloves were stiff, heavy, and uncomfortable. Today's gloves fit so well and are so flexible and light that altering them only decreases their dexterity and protection.

This protective glove (BRINE's Deft™) is made for both men and women, and has an adjustable free floating wrist guard, dual density foam fingers, and molded Supafly™ Thumb design. (First pictured women's version, second pictured men's version.)

THE HELMET

Like the armor worn by ancient warriors, the lacrosse helmet is designed to withstand battle on the field. Stiff checks, flying sticks, and hard shots mandate a protective helmet equipped with face mask, chin pad, and a cupped four-point chin strap. Make sure the chin strap is fastened to all four hookups to prevent serious injury. All players must wear helmets, and all facemasks must be NOCSAE (National Operating Committee on Standards for Athletic Equipment) approved. Unlike the helmets of old, modern day lacrosse helmets are lightweight, strong, and provide excellent visibility. At an average price of $120, it is an expense that will prove worth its weight in gold.

Field helmets, you will notice, differ somewhat from indoor helmets. Field helmets have a visor and side protection that surpass that of the hockey-style headgear worn indoors.

PADS AND SUCH

Other pieces of protective equipment now mandated for lacrosse players include arm guard/pad and shoulder pads. All players, with the exception of the goalkeeper, must wear shoulder pads. Shoulder pads are important in protecting the clavicle, sternum, and shoulders of an individual player. Since tackling is not allowed in lacrosse, the shoulder pads used are typically very lightweight and flexible (unlike those used in football). In fact, many professional players never wear them at all, though modern rules state that all players through the collegiate level use them.

Arm pads and rib pads are either strongly recommended or required, depending on the league you play in. Arm pads are just that, pads that use a foam-like material to protect the elbows and arms. Arm guards are typically multi-piece articulated pads that include hard plastic inserts to protect against checks. Both offer excellent protection, and a preference for one over the other will depend on your position and

This women's protective pad (BRINE's Eraser BP) has dual-density protection with an internal plate system in high-impact areas. It's designed to fit anatomically and includes the Ventilator™ moisture-management performance liner.

BRINE's new men's helmet, Triumph™, includes a Tru-Fit™ memory foam liner and their Custom 360™ dial fit system for a close fit on any head.

Because the women's game is designed by the rules to be less of a contact sport than the men's, helmets are typically not used. Instead, protective eyewear such as BRINE's Vantage are utilized.

This men's protective pad (BRINE's Menace SP) has a molded armor cap system in shoulder areas, dual-density foam, and an internal plate system in high-impact zones. The upper arm guards are adjustable and removable, and it includes the Ventilator™ moisture-management performance liner.

A STUDY co-authored by Richard Hinton, an executive committee member of the US Lacrosse Sports Science and Safety Committee, concerning lacrosse injuries in high-school-aged boys and girls was published in the September 2005 issue of the *American Journal of Sports Medicine*. The study, the research for which was funded by US Lacrosse, represents the most comprehensive analysis of high school lacrosse injuries ever compiled. Its findings conclude that both boys' and girls' lacrosse are relatively safe sports, with most injuries involving sprains, strains, contusions, and abrasions. The study also found that the overall injury rates for boys' and girls' high school lacrosse were significantly lower than those at the collegiate level.

"This is a landmark publication for the sport," said Steve Stenersen, executive director of US Lacrosse. "In order to properly address injuries within the sport we need reliable data from all levels of play. This study is one of many initiatives that our Sports Science and Safety Committee has undertaken to help make the sport safer." Data for the study was collected from the US Lacrosse-supported Injury Tracking Treatment System of the Fairfax County (Virginia) Public School System from 1999-2001, as well as from the Elite 300 (girls) and Top 205 (boys) summer lacrosse camps in 1999, 2000, and 2001. Data collection has continued in the ensuing years. For boys' high school lacrosse the most common injury was an ankle ligament sprain, resulting from indirect forces (non-contact mechanisms such as cutting and dodging). The second most common injury was a concussive event, caused by legal body-to-body contact or object-to-body contact. The most severe injuries in terms of days lost were ligament sprains to the knee and fractures of the hand or wrist.

For girls' high school lacrosse the most common injury was also an ankle ligament sprain. The head and face area was also one of the primary injury areas for girls, but contusions rather than concussive events were the more common injury type. The data for this study predates the use of protective eyewear in women's lacrosse, which was recommended by US Lacrosse for 2004 and mandated beginning in 2005. The most common severe injuries in terms of time lost were also fractures of the wrist and ligament sprains of the knee.

The injury rate for boys (2.89 per 1,000 athletic exposures) was slightly higher than that for girls (2.54). Boys were more often injured during games, but girls were more likely to be injured in practice situations.

preference. Some modern players also opt for rib pads for additional protection in that region.

Other recommended equipment includes athletic supporters and protective cups. Any type of protective cup will work, though some modern designs are more comfortable and protective, specifically the latest compression short cup combo from Shock Doctor.

The goalkeeper is required to wear a throat protector and chest protector, in addition to a helmet, mouthpiece, and gloves. A mouthpiece is also mandatory for all players and must be a highly visible color.

FOOTWEAR

With the recent entrance of Nike, Addidas, Reebok, and New Balance into lacrosse sportswear, the development of lacrosse cleats is proceeding with leaps and bounds. Look forward in the near future to when these companies' research and development labs come up with high-tech footwear designed specifically for the rigors of the lacrosse field or floor. Lacrosse cleats are currently being produced by Brine, Addidas, Reebok, and Warrior (New Balance), though any functional pair of cleats will do. Players will want to avoid playing in non-cleated shoes, unless playing on artificial turf.

CHAPTER 6

WARMING UP: TEN CORE WARM-UP EXERCISES

One of the most important and often overlooked aspects of athletic training is the warm-up. Many players and coaches rush through this part of practice so that time can be spent on skills training and game practice. The warm-up, however, is an indispensable part of developing a healthy and injury-free player. If done correctly, it will significantly add to a player's ability. Traditional training modes mandates a pretraining warm-up devoted to static stretches. This is something to be avoided. Performing static or traditional stretching as a warm-up can actually increase the rate of injury. It is better to use movements and exercises that closely resemble that activities that are about to take place. For example, to warm up for running, it is best to begin by walking, then slowly increase the movement intensity until it becomes a jog and then a run. This way you are preparing the body to perform specific motions. To that end our warm ups use movements similar to those that will be performed on the field—running, throwing, catching, and dodging. This prepares the body to do what it will be asked to do as a player on the lacrosse field. In addition to warming you up, it also works to help develop muscle memory for moves such as face dodges and ground balls.

WARM-UP

The warm-up should be a core warm-up that involves the whole body. It will consist of a series of dynamic movements, some of which mimic movements that the body will perform in a game. It will include yoga movements and calisthenics, followed by 10-15 minutes of exercises called "How to Run" drills. These exercises are specifically designed to warm up the legs of a player while working on developing better form in running. Together they provide a holistic approach to preparing players for the rigors of the sport and help to increase their running ability.

Core Warm-Up

A basic dynamic warm up will begin with a light jog or calisthenics, such as jumping jacks. If using the jog as a warm-up, start by walking around the track or field, slowly increasing the pace to a fast jog by the end of the lap. If indoors or not at a track, substitute a 10-20 rep set of four-count jumping jacks or some similar exercise. Immediately after the jog or jumping jacks, begin the following exercises.

THE DANGERS OF STRETCHING

"Make sure to stretch before training" is advice heard often in gyms around the country. Many Americans think of stretching as the start of any exercise. If your muscles feel tight, stretching is usually the prescription. But is it good for you? Does it help with recovery and alleviate aches and pains? Most controversial of all, does it really increase flexibility? Some recent research may indicate exactly the opposite.

Studies of stretching done over the years have yielded some surprising results. Indeed, there is really very little scientific information demonstrating that static stretching is a good method for increasing flexibility. In fact, there's quite a bit of evidence showing it may be harmful. Donald Murphy, D.C., (in "A Critical Look at Static Stretching: Are We Doing Our Patients Harm?" from *Chiropractic Sports Medicine*, Volume 5, Number 3, 1991) questions the different reasons why people stretch and argues that those reasons are not necessarily valid.

A study by the United States military showed that static stretching performed before exercise actually increased the rate of injury. Note that the method of stretching described, static stretching, is the most common activity among active people. By comparison, other methods of stretching, such as dynamic and isometric stretches, have been associated with much lower injury rates.

The most frequent reason people give for stretching is to prevent injury. Both the military study and Murphy's studies show the opposite: Static stretching can increase the risk of injury! This is because many people stretch their muscles to the point of pain. Pain is your body's message to stop because you are about to cause injuries. When cold muscles are stretched this way, they tend to tear slightly, and this causes small amounts of scar tissue that are not particularly flexible and thus further impede flexibility. One muscle group that the Murphy study focuses on is the hamstring muscles. The hamstrings are both the most frequently injured and the most stretched muscles. Many people insist that stretching prevents injury by increasing their flexibility or range of motion. This may be true. But the cost may be muscle tightness or decreased muscle ability (hypo-activity), increasing the possibility of injury. The types of injury created by stretching may be in the muscle itself, in the tendon and ligament associated with that muscle, and/or even in the joint controlled by that muscle.

If you exercise, the warm-up is vital. It increases blood flow through the muscles, preparing them to work better. Contrary to popular belief, stretching does not do this, so it should not be classified as a warm-up. Stretching while a muscle is cold is the number one route to injuring that muscle group. In addition many people use stretching to "cool down." While this activity may help you to cool down, due to its lack of intensity, it does not help to prevent muscle soreness or injury. Simply put, the best way to warm up and cool down is by a gradual increase and decrease of exercise intensity and range of motion. This should be done by performing movements that you will be doing while participating in the planned activity. For example, if you plan to run, it is best to warm up by walking and slowly increasing your pace to a run. Your cool down reverses the process, gradually decreasing your pace to a walk.

Many athletes stretch, thinking it will help their performance. But studies have shown this is not the case. Flexibility derived from proper warm-up and cool-down, proper form and relaxation is the key and may be achieved without using potentially harmful static stretches. Dynamic warm-up and cool-down movements that mimic the moves to be performed on the field are the number one way to increase flexibility and performance while decreasing injury.

Neck Rotations

This will warm the neck muscles while allowing the body to get used to the additional weight of the headgear if done wearing a helmet.

Be cognizant of any areas of tightness or impingement. Perform 5-10 rotations to the right and then to the left.

Step 1. Stand with your feel shoulder width apart.

Step 2. Begin a slow and controlled 360-degree headroll, increasing the range of motion with every revolution.

Shoulder Rotations

Shoulder injuries are the number one upper body injury in lacrosse. Having strong and healthy shoulder joints is a must. When done properly, these exercises will help to strengthen the shoulder joint while keeping it limber, helping to prevent potential injuries.

Step 1. With your stick in one hand extend your arm out to your side at a 90-degree angle.

Step 2. Slowly make a small, controlled circle with your hand while keeping your stick vertical to the ground. Concentrate on making a full circle about 10 inches in diameter.

Step 3. Perform this exercise with your arm extended to the side, to the front, overhead and to the rear.

Be cognizant of any areas of tightness or impingement. Perform 5-10 reps to each side and in each direction.

Arm Twists

Step 1. Stand with your stick held vertically in one hand and extended out from your side at a 90-degree angle.

Step 2. Begin a slow and controlled rotation of your hand, wrist, and arm as if dumping the ball out of your stick. Rotate your hand as far forward as it will go while keeping your arm straight, turning the butt-end of the stick to the sky.

Step 3. Reverse direction rotating your hand, wrist, and arm as far back as you can in an attempt to point the butt-end of the stick to the sky.

Be aware of any areas of tightness or impingement. Perform 5-10 reps with each hand.

Face Dodge Trunk Twister

Step 1. Hold your stick in a two-hand cradle position.

Step 2. Rotate your trunk to the opposite side of your body while letting your stick travel with you. Completely rotate your trunk so that your stick ends up on the opposite side of your body with the head of the stick by your ear.

Step 3. Return to the starting position.

Be cognizant of any areas of tightness or impingement. Perform 5-10 reps on each side.

D-Squats

Step 1. Stand with your feet shoulder width apart and with your stick in an upright position.

Step 2. Step out to one side, squatting into a defensive position while extending your stick as if to give a poke check.

Step 3. Return to the starting position and perform to the opposite side.

Be aware of any areas of tightness or impingement. Perform 5-10 reps to each side, dropping lower with each repetition to gain full range of motion.

Ground Ball Stoke

Step 1. Stand with your stick to one side of your body.

Step 2. Squat down while allowing your arms to swing the stick like a shovel toward the ground as if you were picking up a ground ball.

Step 3. Stand back up with your stick upright and in front of your face.

Make sure to get low enough to scrape your gloves on the ground. Be cognizant of any areas of tightness or impingement. Perform 5-10 reps to each side.

Face-Off Lunge

Step 1. Begin standing with your stick parallel to the ground.

Step 2. Squat down as if facing off and extend one leg back as far as you can while keeping your gloves and stick on the ground.

Step 3. Return to a standing position.

Step 4. Repeat with the other leg.

Be aware of any areas of tightness or impingement. Perform 5-10 reps with each leg.

Drop and Push

Step 1. Assume a push-up position.

Step 2. While keeping your arms extended and locked, drop your hips toward the floor and pull your head back, nose to the sky.

Step 3. Drop your head back to the ground and, while keeping your legs straight, push your buttocks up into the air forming an upside-down V with your body.

Be cognizant of any areas of tightness or impingement. Perform 5-10 reps.

Scorpions

Step 1. Lie flat on your belly with your arms extended out 90 degrees from your body.

Step 2. While keeping your arms and upper body on the ground, rotate your foot up and toward the opposite hand, letting your hips rise off the ground if necessary.

Step 3. Rotate back down and return to the starting position.

Step 4. Repeat on opposite side.

Be aware of any areas of tightness or impingement Perform 5-10 reps per side.

Cat Stretch

Step 1. Begin on all fours

Step 2. Push your midback up to the sky trying to round your back as much as possible.

Step 3. Allow your abdomen to drop back down toward the floor and push toward the floor.

Be cognizant of any areas of tightness or impingement. Perform 5 reps.

CHAPTER 7

FINISHING THE WARM-UP: HOW-TO-RUN EXERCISES

You've completed the ten core warm-up exercises. Excellent! We'll finish your warm-up in a minute with some precision running drills, but let's pause to review a few points. A thorough warm-up should be performed before any and all exercises, whether in the gym or on the field or track. It should become a standard and an automatic thing for you to prepare yourself for the training/practice/game that will follow. Pay attention to how your body feels before you start. If you feel "cold," or if a specific muscle group is "tight" or sore, continue working it, using the movements you've just learned, until the area feels properly warm and loose. Be aware of what you need to do prepare your body, and give any problem area the additional attention it needs.

Coaches should allow an additional five minutes or so after the set warm up for each player to address his or her individual needs. This will allow each player the time to customize his or her warm-up and properly prepare for an injury-free game or practice. Remember, a proper warm-up will prime your pump for the workouts to come and is critical to avoiding injuries.

HOW-TO-RUN EXERCISES

These exercises, as the final part of the warm-up, are intended to be performed before any activity that will include running or track work, in practice or in a game. They should also be performed prior to weight training, though it is not absolutely mandatory to do so. Take the time to develop good technique so that you get the maximum benefit from the movements you're performing. These exercises break up the running stride into its component parts and allow a player to fully prepare his or her legs for the rigors of practice or play. Remember, these exercises are about warming up the body and are not a pure conditioning exercise. How fast or hard a player does these exercises is not so important as how well they do them. Proper form and good mechanics are paramount.

Why do how-to-run exercises? Though it may sound incredible, many athletes do not know how to run properly. That is to say, their running form is inefficient. The how-to-run exercises break down each part of the running stride in a way that allows for correcting any particular part of the running stride. This, combined with proper spinal alignment and arm swing, can transform a mediocre runner into a star. At the very least it will help to increase the efficiency and comfort of your running stride. Perform these exercises over a 10-15 yard running area or on a track. Do not run on cement or concrete if possible, because these surfaces are too hard and can add to injury potential. If you are running on a track or path, wear appropriate running shoes made by a reputable manufacturer. Ideally, you should run on a grass or turf field, wearing the cleats or turf shoes that you would wear if playing in a game or at practice. Perform the following exercises in the order indicated, as they are incremental and sequential.

Toe Pops

This isolates the initial movement of a running step, the push off with the ball of the foot. To perform a toe pop, keep your legs straight and bound off the ball of the foot landing on the opposite foot. Use only the balls of the feet to propel yourself, making sure to not let your heels touch the ground or to bend your legs too much. Strive for perfect form. Perform this 1-3 times.

Skips

Just like it sounds, it is a skip that represents the continuation of the initial explosion of force in a stride. Be sure to swing your opposite arm in counterbalance to the skip. The goal of this is to get a high springing step driving your body up and off the ground. Strive for perfect form. Perform this 1-3 times.

High Knees

Keeping your back straight and head up, start a light jog while bringing each knee up as high as possible. Keep your arms swinging. Strive for perfect form. Perform this 1-3 times.

Kick Out

At the top of the high knee stride, kick your lower leg out at a 90-degree angle to your body, pointing the ball of the foot and extending the leg as far forward as possible. Strive for perfect form. Perform this 1-3 times.

Butt Kickers

Quickly and rapidly bring the heels up toward the buttocks, as if you were trying to kick yourself in the bottom with your heels. Try to kick up the grass in your wake. Strive for perfect form. Perform this 1-3 times.

CHAPTER 8
AGILITY TRAINING

Agility training is extremely important in any running and cutting sport. Lacrosse is essentially that, so these drills are paramount in developing a great lacrosse player. Agility training should take place at least three times a week when the athletes are fresh and properly warmed up. Some coaches even use an entire practice dedicated to both agility and stick drills, so every player can get this training in while under supervision and guidance. Keep in mind as you run these drills that perfecting technique is the major goal, not conditioning. Coaches and assistant coaches should act as monitors for each drill and give constructive criticism on the performance of each individual player.

Agility training must not be attempted without an adequate warm-up. Performing agility and speed training while the body is still fresh is also very important. Though this type of training has a conditioning component, it is still predominantly a skill in development. The body learns best when it is rested, so it is imperative that players work on skill development before hard practice or conditioning. Fatigue should not become a mitigating factor in learning these skills and developing proper form. It takes thousands of perfect repetitions of any one move to obtain perfect muscle memory. Therefore, when performing these drills, perfection in technique is paramount.

Keep in mind as you work through the drills that follow that they are actually base skill drills that can be layered with additional skills after players become competent with the initial moves. For example, you can place a ground ball at the top of the split drill and a goal past the demarcating cone. The player will then pick up a ground ball, perform the split, and fire a shot on the run to end the drill. This allows coaches and players to increase the complexity of the drills as ability increases while being very time efficient in practice sessions. Use your imagination when adding on variable skills, remembering to only add an additional layer of complexity after the initial base skill is completely and accurately absorbed by the players.

If an agility ladder or cones are available, use them; if not, utilize the players' sticks by laying them parallel to one another with a foot or two between the sticks creating a ladder. The drills are broken up into two parts: ladders and slaloms, and box drills. Each will help to develop field-applicable abilities in a player and should be looked on as an integral art of developing skill, conditioning, and ability.

These drills are serious workouts in themselves. They can be performed as part of a warm up or as a separate agility session. Once a player has mastered the techniques involved, other skills can be layered on these drills. At the higher levels two players can perform a mirror image of these drills, one being an offensive player and the other defensive. This adds game context to such drills and helps the player to understand their use in a game. As a coach it is important to be creative and keep drills interesting and relevant to the players and the game.

LADDERS AND SLALOM

Set up cones, ladder, or sticks on the ground over a 10-15 yard area. Make sure the sticks are lined up and equally spaced if using this method. Take care that no player steps on another player's stick; this way we prevent both potential injury and equipment breakage. Here are the basic drills.

Two Steps In

Step 1. Stand facing the bottom of the ladder.

Step 2. Keep your head held high and use your peripheral vision to see the ladder. Using a high knee stride, place one foot into the first rung of the ladder.

Step 3. Using a high knee stride, place your other foot into the same rung of the ladder as your initial step.

Step 4. Continue this high knee double-step, landing both feet in each rung before moving on to the next.

Step 5. Continue for the full length of the ladder.

Strive for light, fast steps and quickness. Keep the arms pumping as well. Perform this 1-5 times.

Two Steps In

Two Steps In/Two Steps Out

Step 1. Face one side of the ladder.

Step 2. Using the foot nearest the top of the ladder, step into the first rung.

Step 3. Step the trailing foot in the same rung next to the first foot.

Step 4. Now step the first foot back out followed by the trailing foot.

Step 5. Continue with each successive rung for the fill length of the ladder.

Perform this 1-5 times.

Two Steps In/Two Steps Out

Slalom Run (version one)

If you are using the players' sticks, line them up ladder-style. If using cones, place cones in a zigzag formation, keeping the angle between each rather acute.

Step 1. Race to the first cone.

Step 2. Perform a hop-switch (see sidebar) that swivels your hips toward the second cone.

Step 3. Sprint to the second cone.

Step 4. Repeat all the way up the full length of the slalom course/ladder.

Perform 1-5 times.

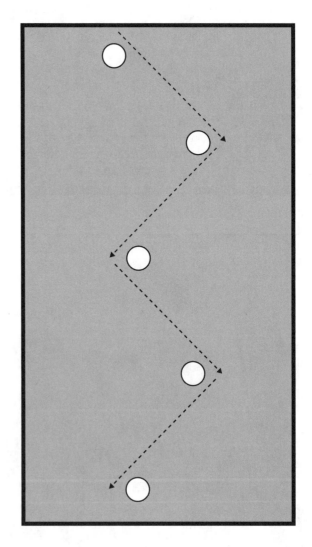

THE HOP-SWITCH

The hop-switch is a unique method for changing directions while running. It is different from a traditional change of direction move in that it takes the braking force off of the outside foot and places it on the inboard foot, leaving the outside foot light. This allows the outside foot to be used to spring into the next sprint. It takes some practice, but when done correctly it is faster, easier, and less injurious than traditional methods of cutting.

To perform the hop-switch, run toward a cone. When your reach the cone, take a little hop into the air. While air-borne rotate your hips in the direction that you want to go next. This switching of the hips prepositions your feet in the next direction of movement. When you hit the ground, explode into a sprint. This method is derived from kinesthetic studies and practical application in sports. It is the fastest method to change direction. Due to the balance hop and prepositioning of the power source, legs, and hips, in the next direction of movement, the cut is made faster with less stress placed on the outside knee. This method first made its debut on the basketball court where knee injuries from quick cutting is prevalent and a fast first step is essential.

Slalom Run (version two)

This is done in much the same way as version one except that instead of performing a hop-switch facing the cone, you will perform one that places your back toward it as if doing a roll dodge.

Step 1. Run toward the first cone.

Step 2. Perform a hop-switch, turning your back to the cone.

Step 3. Accelerate from the first cone and run to the second one.

Step 4. Perform a second hop-switch.

Step 5. Continue through the entire slalom/ladder.

Perform 1-5 times.

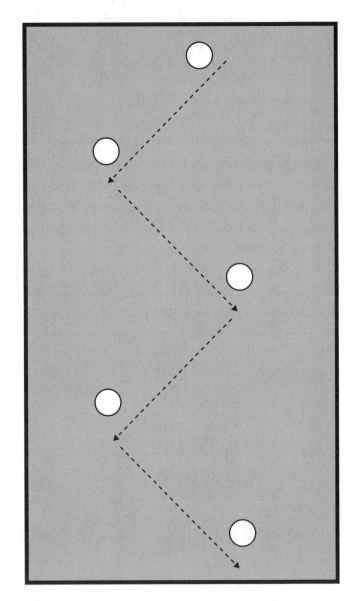

Forward and Back

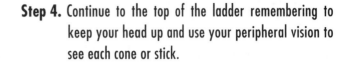

Step 1. Begin by facing one side of the slalom/ladder.

Step 2. Sprint forward to the first cone, rounding it at the tip.

Step 3. Run backwards to the second cone, rounding it at the base.

Step 4. Continue to the top of the ladder remembering to keep your head up and use your peripheral vision to see each cone or stick.

Perform this 1-5 times.

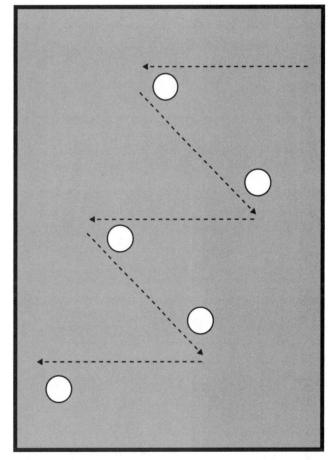

Split Drill

Place a single cone in front of a player or coach.

Step 1. Run directly toward this cone from about 10 yards away.

Step 2. Perform a hop-switch just before the cone, prepositioning your hips/feet.

Step 3. Accelerate to one side or the other sprinting past the cone or another 5 yards or so.

Perform 1-5 times.

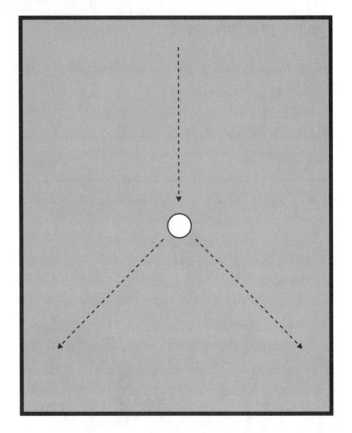

THE agility drills in this book are designed to be progressive in nature and to mimic moves that will be performed while playing. This allows a coach to add variables to the drills as players' skills increase. For example, once a player is proficient with the hop-switch in the slalom drills, you should add the variable of the stick in hand to the drill. Have players perform a stick protection move (face, split, belt buckle) at each point of direction change. Be sure to focus on proper stick protection when adding this. After this level of complexity is mastered, add a ground ball pick up prior to running the slalom and a pass off or shot at he end of it.

This is only one example of the levels of complexity and variables that can be added to the base drill. Use your imagination and creativity when adding these additions to the base drill, being certain that what is added is indeed applicable on the field. This "open variable" drill base can be custom tailored to each player once the base footwork is mastered. For example, if a player has trouble transitioning from a one-hand cradle to a prethrow two-hand cradle, then have him run the drill switching from one to two hands as he hits each cone. If a player has trouble performing a V-cut to get open for a feed, then have him hit a cone, hop-switch, and catch a pass from a player outside the ladder at each alternating cone. The only caveat is not to add a level of complexity or further variables until the base movement, in this case the hop-switch, is completely mastered. That way the brain and body are only processing one new variable. This will prevent players from becoming confused or frustrated, especially with youth-level players.

This method of using a universal base drill and them customizing it to fit an individual player or team need allows a coach to "multitask" in the area of skills training. In addition, it is a time efficient way to give players individual attention while training the team as a whole. Once developed to a level of full interactivity with footwork, dodging and shooting in place can give the entire team a way to train with minimal downtime for the individual player. Interaction is the name of the game, and using a layered approach to developing game abilities will help create players who are comfortable doing multiple tasks while moving aggressively. This can be applied to slalom runs, ladders, and box drill.

BOX DRILLS

Another set of drills that are used to develop lacrosse specific moves and agility are box drills. These use a square running area designated by four sticks or cones placed 5-8 yards apart. Players run to each point at which they change direction and the stride method is then applied. For example, you might sprint to the first corner of the box in a normal run, then turn and use a side shuffle step to get to the next corner, then sprint backwards to the next, run sideways to the last cone, and then a full sprint out of the box. These drills simulate many situations in lacrosse, such as playing defense or driving on goal. Remember, the drills are predominantly skills to be learned properly, so good execution is still the main focus, though conditioning is an inevitable by-product when running these drills hard.

There are four basic box drills: the forward run/lateral run, forward run/lateral shuffle, and the diagonal forward and diagonal backward. As the skills of the individual player increase, add sticks and even a second person in the box to "play against."

Forward Run/Lateral Run

Step 1. Begin at the bottom left cone.

Step 2. Sprint to the top left cone.

Step 3. Hop-switch to your right and run to the top right hand cone.

Step 4. Hop-switch again and backward sprint to the bottom right cone.

Step 5. Hop-switch again and run to your starting position.

Step 6. Hop-switch again and sprint out of the box completely.

Make sure to stay facing the top of the box the entire time. Perform this 1-5 times.

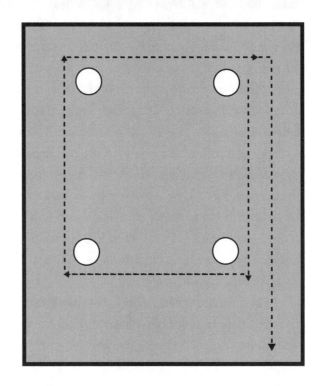

Forward Run/Lateral Shuffle

Step 1. Begin at the bottom left cone.

Step 2. Sprint to the top left cone.

Step 3. Keeping your hips facing forward, shuffle laterally to the top right cone.

Step 4. Sprint backwards to the bottom right cone.

Step 5. Keeping your hips facing forward, shuffle laterally to your starting position.

Step 6. Sprint toward the top left cone and out of the box completely.

Perform this 1-5 times.

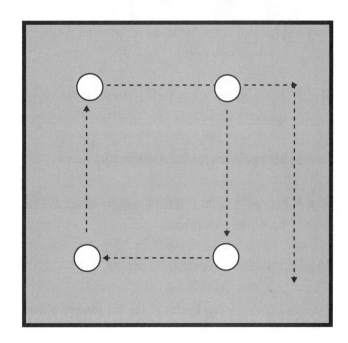

Diagonal Forward

Step 1. Beginning at the bottom left cone, sprint diagonally to the top right cone.

Step 2. Hop-switch and run or shuffle laterally to the top left cone.

Step 3. Hop-switch and run to the bottom right cone.

Step 4. Hop-switch at the bottom right cone and run or shuffle to your starting point.

Step 5. Hop-switch and sprint out to the box.

Be careful to stay facing the top of the box the entire time. Perform this 1-5 times.

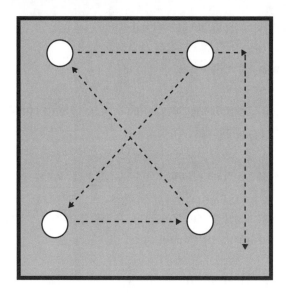

Diagonal Backwards

Step 1. Beginning at the top left cone, sprint diagonally to the bottom right cone.

Step 2. Hop-switch and run or shuffle laterally to the bottom left cone.

Step 3. Hop-switch and run diagonally to the top right cone.

Step 4. Hop-switch at the bottom right cone and sprint out to the box.

Be careful to stay facing the top of the box the entire time. Perform this 1-5 times.

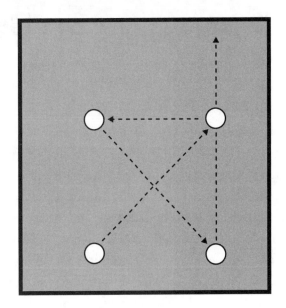

CHAPTER 9

PREPARATIONS FOR PROPER STRENGTH TRAINING

Many methods and styles of weight training have been popularized by the fitness industry. Most have some merit, but keep in mind that the fitness industry's primary focus is on the development of an aesthetically pleasing body, not on superior athletic performance. The methods described in this book are concerned solely with developing strength and explosiveness, building core body balance, and limiting injuries. We are not interested in how big you can build your biceps or how much you can bench. Keep the distinction between athletic and aesthetic training in mind when you wonder why we've omitted some favorite, and added some completely new, exercises to your training.

KNOW your muscle types. Athletic training is focused on developing fast-twitch muscle fibers for explosive movements and dynamic body strength. It utilizes exercises that demand a neurological and systemic response from the body that translates into performance outside the weight room. Aesthetic training is focused on hypertrophy, or the building of the size of the muscle, and body fat levels in order to show them off. Muscle size and strength are not the same. Raw strength and functional strength are also not the same.

Athletic training must be periodized, as trainers say. This means the primary goal is to build a base of raw strength. At the same time we use explosive movements to encourage proper neural and muscular development. The functional muscles of athletes are macroscopically different in their capillary development from those of bodybuilders.

Athletic training's second focus is on balancing the dominant/non-dominant sides of the body to spread that functional strength out equally. This division of the training allows you to focus on one aspect of training at a time to obtain maximum results. The body is an incredibly adaptive machine, but it adapts best to one set of stimuli at a time. That is why the program is broken up as it is. This progressive and synergistic method truly is the ultimate path to total lacrosse conditioning.

Strength training for lacrosse is similar to the training for any other dynamic contact sport. Any player in any sport needs to develop the functional strength that will translate into maximum performance on the field. The strength training sessions that this book describes are designed with those results in mind. The programs are broken up into:

- Preseason Strength
- Preseason Explosive
- Preseason Balance
- In-Season Maintenance
- Postseason Recovery

Each of these five programs will deliver something a bit different to the player. Combining these methods as you prep for and then begin your season will maximize your results on the field. Remember, what you do in the weight room will determine what you can do on the field.

Bigger, stronger, and faster is the name of the game in most sports these days. Indeed, if you want to play at the Division 1 or professional level of lacrosse, you will need to become an exceptional athlete. The average D-1 player today is 6 feet tall, weighs 200 plus pounds and has a 40-yard dash time that would leave some track stars envious. Add to that the cardiovascular fitness of a soccer player, the hand-eye coordination of a tennis player, the physicality of a footballer, and the field sense and offensive maneuvering of a basketball star, and you get an all-around athlete that is hard to compete with. Train properly with weights and on the proper schedule, and your program will help you attain a higher level of athleticism. Remember, muscle size is not the goal. Functional strength is.

EQUIPMENT

For the type of strength training you will be engaged in it is vital to have the right equipment available. Make sure your gym has the following equipment before beginning these programs: Olympic bar, physio-ball, medicine ball (synthetic), dumbbells or kettlebells, Olympic weights, adjustable bench, squat rack with keepers, pull up bar, Olympic lifting platform, free-motion cable machine, hex bar, and a hyperextension chair. If it does not have the adequate equipment, find a training center that does. Typically, strength and conditioning centers at competitive community colleges or universities will have everything you need.

In addition, it is recommended that you wear proper shoes while lifting. Wear a cross-training, wrestling, or power-lifting shoe. Running shoes are not proper footwear for weight training. Running shoes are not designed for lateral stability, and lifting heavy weights with them will diminish their useful life. Weight belts and wrist wraps are also not recommended because they do not allow for true strength-based development and are essentially a crutch. Professional weight lifters have a motto: If you can't hold it, you can't lift it. Not using a weight belt in particular is why getting proper instruction and using perfect form while training is so important. It really is easy to injure yourself handling weights in the wrong way.

BREATHING EXERCISES

There are many schools of thought as to how you should breathe while lifting weights. Indeed, there is even a school that uses breathing techniques to provide what is called a "virtual" weight belt while lifting heavy weights. No matter what method you use, keep breathing throughout your training. Your body will only work properly when given adequate air intake. Learn to get into a rhythm while training. When lifting moderate or lighter weights, it is okay to breathe out while on the load side of a lift. Pressing a weight overhead is on the load side. When lifting heavy weights, the opposite may be more beneficial. By breathing in you expand and support the body in the load phase.

Experiment with both and be sure to feel how it affects your lifts. Use the technique that gives you the best results. While resting between sets, use a slow breathing technique, drawing in air using your diaphragm and filling the lower part of your lungs first. Breathe deeply and smoothly to control the rate of respiration. Ten deeps breaths just prior to and following a lift can give you a distinct power boost as oxygen is pumped back into your system.

HOW TO CALCULATE 1RM

Find the number of reps to concentric (positive) failure that you can perform with a certain weight. For example, if while benching you can only do eight reps with a certain weight and could not possibly perform another rep with proper form, then that is your point of failure. Now take that number and cross-reference it with the following table. For example, if you can do 3 reps to failure with 135 pounds, then the percentage of 1 rep max that represents is 78 percent.

Next, divide the weight that you can do by that percentage using decimals (78 percent equals 0.78), and that will give you an approximation of your one repetition maximum. For example, if you can perform 8 reps with 135 pounds in the bench press, that means that 135 pounds is 78 percent (0.78) of your one repetition maximum. So you would take 135 divided by 0.78 and that would equal 173 pounds. Your 1 rep max will be your guideline for determining the amount of weight you will be attempting to lift in any given workout. It will also be your measurement of increased strength as you become stronger during each training session. It is a great way to measure your progress and a good stat to have for any recruiting efforts you may be doing.

REPS%	1RM
1	100
2	95
3	90
4	88
5	86
6	83
7	80
8	78
9	76
10	75
11	72
12	70

CHAPTER 10

FORTY OF THE BEST STRENGTH-TRAINING EXERCISES

This chapter will give you a first look at 40 of the best strength-training exercises for lacrosse. These exercises will form the core of your strength training. Many of these exercises are not part of the normal repertoire offered by fitness trainers, so it is important that you seek additional instruction from a qualified strength and conditioning coach if questions arise. A qualified coach is someone with the proper background, including certification from the National Strength and Conditioning Association, the Collegiate Strength and Conditioning Coaches Association, or the National College of Sports Medicine. A basic certification in personal training or some experience in bodybuilding is not a sufficient background for advanced athletic training. Seek out proper advice and ask your gym whether you will be allowed to perform the ballistic exercises we prescribe. In addition, make sure to wear proper footwear and attire for the training and always observe proper gym etiquette. Remember, as a lacrosse player you are an ambassador for the sport.

Bench Press

Step 1. Lie flat on a bench with your feet flat on the floor. A barbell should be placed on the holding rack just above you. Grasp the bar with an overhand grip slightly more than shoulder width apart.

Step 2. Lift the bar off the rack until your arms are fully extended.

Step 3. In a controlled motion, lower the bar until your upper arms are parallel to the floor and your forearms are at a 90-degree angle to your upper arms, come to a complete stop.

Step 4. Push the bar back up to full extension in line with your chin.

Step 5. Repeat for the prescribed number of reps in the set.

Lateral Raise

Step 1. Stand upright with a dumbbell in each hand and with your palms in toward your body.

Step 2. While keeping your arms straight, raise the weights simultaneously out to your sides until your hands are slightly above your shoulders with your thumbs slightly tilted toward the floor (as if pouring tea).

Step 3. Hold at the top of the motion for an instant and slowly lower the weights back to the starting position.

Proper Squat Form

Though one of the most beneficial lifting movements you can do, the squat is often a source of nightmarish stories of career-ending injuries. This is largely due to the improper performance of the motion itself. When done properly, the squat is the single best exercise for an athlete to perform. To squat properly and safely, begin by positioning the bar on your trapezius muscle and rolling it "one notch down." This should take it to the middle of your shoulder blades, where powerlifters also prefer it. This is the recommended technique because it gives you a better spinal alignment and keeps the weight in line with your heels when you squat.

Once under the bar, keep your head up with your eyes facing straight ahead. Your hands should be placed wide on the bar for support, your feet slightly more than shoulder width apart, and your toes tuned out slightly. Push your chest out while pulling your shoulders back and begin "sitting back" as if sitting down in a chair. Do not allow your knees to bend forward and out over your feet. This will cause undo stress on your knees and lead to injury. Tighten your abs and you lower your body until your thighs are parallel to the ground. Hold this position for an instant and then begin your movement back up to your starting position. A spotter and the use of a power rack or cage are highly recommended.

Test out your squat form by placing a bar a few inches in front or your shins just below your knees. Perform a squat using your body weight only, making sure your shins do not touch the bar as you descend and ascend. If they do, then you are allowing your knees to bend forward and out over your feet. This is a recipe for injury. Use this method to perfect your squat technique before you begin lifting heavy weights. Use your spotter or a mirror to check your form.

Squat

Step 1. Begin with your feet shoulder width apart with barbell resting on your upper back and traps. Your hands should grasp the bar in an overhand grip.

Step 2. Keeping your head up, back straight, and chest out, slowly lower the weight by bending your knees and sitting back until your thighs are parallel to the floor. Be careful not to allow your knees to come out over your feet. (This will cause undue strain on your knee joint.)

Step 3. Push through your heels and stand up. Do not bounce the weight as you stand.

Rows

Step 1. Holding either a barbell or dumbbells stand with your knees shoulder width apart and slightly bent. Chin up, back straight, and chest out. Bend at the waist to a 90-degree angle and grasp the weights with your arms hanging in front of you.

Step 2. Keeping your body locked, pull the weights slowly toward your stomach, squeezing your shoulder blades together as you do so.

Step 3. Stop for an instant at the top of the motion and slowly lower the weight back down to the starting position.

Deadlift

Step 1. Stand with your feet shoulder-width apart. Your chin is up, your back straight, and your chest is out. Bending your legs, reach down and grasp the barbell in an overhand grip.

Step 2. Keeping your arms extended, push through your heels and stand up, concentrating on using your legs and not your lower back.

Step 3. Slowly lower the bar back to the ground.

THE deadlift is one of the best exercises for developing overall body strength. Like the squat, it is an exercise that taxes the entire body and must be performed with great care and perfect form in order to prevent injury. If it is available, use a hex bar for all deadlifts. This piece of equipment helps to keep the load in line with your body and does not place as much stress on your lower back. Deadlifting with an Olympic bar is much riskier. If a hex bar is not available at your local gym, order one on your own online, or ask the gym manager to get one. It will pay off in the end.

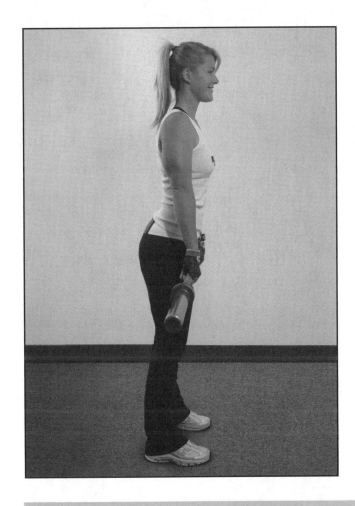

Back Extensions

Step 1. Lie face down on a hyperextension bench.

Step 2. Bend at your waist so that your head hangs toward the ground.

Step 3. Cross your hands in front of your chest and slowly raise your upper body until it is parallel with the floor.

Military Press

Step 1. Stand straight up with a barbell at shoulder level in front of you.

Step 2. Using an overhand grip that is slightly wider than shoulder width, press the weight up over your head until your arms are completely extended. Make sure

that your arms are completely over your head and in line with your ears and not out in front of you.

Step 3. Slowly lower the weight back down to the start position.

Leg Press

Step 1. Sit in a leg press machine, making sure your back is flat against the seatback. Place your feet on the press platform at shoulder width.

Step 2. Slowly lower the weights as far as you can without letting your back arch off the seatback.

Step 3. Hold for an instant and press the weight back extending your legs.

Physio-Ball Push-Ups

Step 1. On an inflatable physio-ball, assume a push-up position with your hands and chest on the ball and your feet on the floor.

Step 2. Keeping your body straight, push into the ball as you lift your upper body off the ball until your arms are extended.

Step 3. Hold for an instant and lower yourself slowly back onto the ball.

Hanging Leg Raises

Step 1. Grasp a pull-up bar with an overhand grip and hang from it.

Step 2. Keep your legs straight and lift them toward your head as you allow the hips to swivel forward.

Step 3. Hold for an instant and then slowly lower your legs back down, being careful not to swing.

Weighted Pull-Ups

You can use a weight belt with a chain attachment to hang additional weight between your legs while performing pull-ups, or simply hold a dumbbell between your thighs (pictured). Make sure your pull-ups covers a full range of motion.

Step 1. Face a pull-up bar gasping it in an overhand grip with your hands slightly more than shoulder width apart. Let your body hang and completely extend your arms. Pull yourself up until your chin clears the bar

Step 2. Hold for an instant and lower yourself back to down to full extension.

Overhead Push-Press

Step 1. Stand straight up with a barbell at your shoulder level in an overhand grip that is slightly wider than shoulder width.

Step 2. Bend your knees in a half squat and explode upward using the momentum to help press the weight up over your head. Keep going until your arms are completely extended.

Step 3. Slowly lower the weight back down to the start position.

Barbell Twists

Step 1. Place a barbell with one end up against a wall or in a corner. Stand to one side of the bar and grasp the end of the bar with both hands.

Step 2. Keep your arms straight while you rotate the bar out in front of you and complete a circle to the other side of your body. Use your core and legs to control the motion.

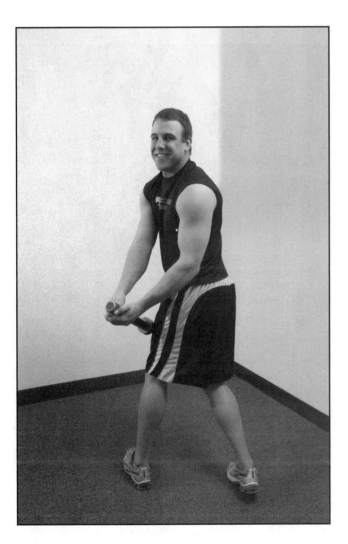

Bottom Squats

Step 1. Using a squat cage or rack, place an Olympic bar at a position equal to the bottom of your squat movement, thighs parallel to the ground.

Step 2. Situate yourself under the bar and explode the weight upward in a controlled but ballistic motion.

Step 3. Lower the weight down slowly and rest the barbell at the bottom position before your next rep.

Bottom Bench

Step 1. Using a squat cage or rack place an Olympic bar in a position that simulates your bottom position in your bench press. Be sure your arms are not bent past a 90-degree angle, for this can cause injury to the shoulder joint.

Step 2. Position yourself under the bar and explode the weight up and off the rack in a controlled ballistic movement.

Step 3. Lower the weight slowly back to the rack, releasing pressure on the bar before your next rep.

Hanging Cleans

Step 1. Begin with a barbell hanging at midthigh, legs bent; chin up and your back straight.

Step 2. Explode up with your legs and pull up with your arms. As the momentum of the weight travels up to shoulder level, quickly drop your elbows to the floor and "catch" the weight, using your legs as a shock absorber.

Step 3. Lower the weight and repeat.

Jerks

Step 1. With a barbell held in front of you at shoulder level, bend your knees slightly and bounce up explosively while splitting your legs. One leg should be forward, the other back, while allowing the momentum of the bounce and split to carry the weight over head. Lock out your arms.

Step 2. Step up into a standing overhead position.

Step 3. Lower the weight and repeat.

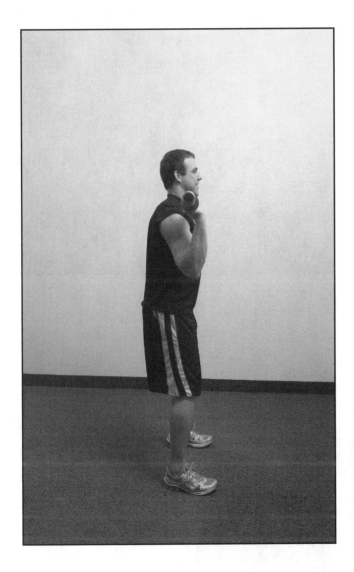

Barbell Snatch

Step 1. Grasp an Olympic bar with a wide grip. Squat down and let the barbell hang about midcalf.

Step 2. Explode upwards, pulling your elbow high and allowing the momentum to carry the barbell overhead in one smooth motion. Lock your arm out in the overhead position.

Step 3. Lower the barbell and repeat.

Plyo-Push-Ups

Step 1. Begin in a push-up position with feet on the floor and hands on a flat bench. Lower yourself slowly to the bench

Step 2. Explode upward, driving your upper body off the bench.

Step 3. Catch yourself as you come back down. Control your descent to the bench and explode up again.

Cable Twists

Step 1. Adjust a cable or free-motion machine so that the pulley is at shoulder level. Stand facing the pulley in an offset stance, and grasp the handle with the arm opposite your front leg.

Step 2. With your arms extended, twist toward your back foot. Allow your feet to pivot in order to get full range of motion.

Step 3. Return to center and repeat.

Make sure you perform this exercise on both sides. Remember to switch your stance accordingly.

Physio-Ball Press

Step 1. Lie with your back on a physio-ball and your feet on the ground. Make sure to line up your upper chest with the midpoint of the ball.

Step 2. With the dumbbells positioned evenly over your chest, push upwards until your arms are fully extended.

Step 3. Slowly lower the dumbbells until your upper arms are parallel to the floor and your forearms are at a 90-degree angle to your upper arms. Come to a complete stop.

One-Legged Deadlift

Step 1. Stand on one leg with dumbbells or kettlebells in each hand.

Step 2. Bend your leg and reach down to the floor.

Step 3. Keeping your arms extended, push through your heel and stand upright. Concentrate on using your leg and not your lower back.

Step 4. Slowly lower the weight back to the ground.

Turkish Get-Up

Step 1. Lie flat on the ground with a light dumbbell or kettlebell in one hand.

Step 2. Extend the dumbbell toward the ceiling, locking out your elbow completely.

Step 3. Keeping the arm with the dumbbell pointed to the sky, get up from the ground and assume a standing position.

Step 4. Keep the dumbbell and arm pointed skyward and return to the starting position.

Alternate Hanging Leg Raises

Step 1. Grasp a pull-up bar with an overhand grip and hang.

Step 2. Keeping your leg straight, lift one up toward your head, letting the other leg hang freely.

Step 3. Hold for an instant and then slowly lower your leg back down, being careful not to swing.

Renegade Rows

Step 1. Take dumbbells or kettlebells in your hands and assume a push-up position. The weights should be shoulder width apart.

Step 2. Balance your upper body over the dumbbells and alternately pull one of the dumbbells to your side. As you pull one elbow back, push the other into the floor.

Step 3. Lower the dumbbell to the floor and repeat with the opposite arm.

Make sure to keep your back straight during this exercise.

Dumbbell Squat Press

Step 1. Take a dumbbell or kettlebell in each hand and hold them close to your body at shoulder level.

Step 2. Keep your elbows in tight and squat down until your thighs are parallel to the floor.

Step 3. Explode up, driving the dumbbells up and over your head.

Step 4. Hold this position for an instant, then slowly lower the dumbbells back to the starting position and repeat.

Dumbbell Cleans

Step 1. Begin with dumbbells or kettlebells hanging at midthigh with legs bent, chin up, and your back straight.

Step 2. Explode up with your legs and pull up with your arms. As the momentum of the weight travels up to shoulder level, quickly drop your elbows to the floor and "catch" the weight, using your legs as a shock absorber.

Step 3. Lower the weights and repeat.

Twisting Hyperextensions

Step 1. Begin with a back extension. Lie face down on a hyperextension bench and bend at your waist so that your head hangs toward the ground.

Step 2. Slowly raise your upper body until it is parallel with the floor. Twist slightly as if trying to face the ceiling.

Step 3. Lower your self to the starting position and repeat with the side.

Twisting Hyperextensions

If this is too easy, hold a medicine ball or light dumbbell in your hand while performing this.

Kettlebell Snatch

Step 1. Grasp a dumbbell or kettlebell with one hand and squat down, letting the weight hang about between your legs.

Step 2. Explode upwards, pulling your elbow high and allowing the momentum to carry the weight overhead in one smooth motion. Lock your arm in the overhead position.

Step 3. Lower the dumbbell and repeat.

Overhead Squat

Step 1. Hold an Olympic bar with a wide overhand grip over your head and stand with your feet wider than shoulder width.

Step 2. Keeping the weight above your head, squat down until your thighs are parallel to the floor.

Step 3. Pushing through your heels, stand back up to the beginning position and repeat.

One-Legged Lateral Raises

Step 1. Stand upright on one foot with a dumbbell in each hand. Your palms should be turned in toward your body.

Step 2. Keeping your arms straight, raise the weights simultaneously out to your sides until your hands are slightly above your shoulders. Your thumbs should be slightly tilted toward the floor (as if pouring tea).

Step 3. Hold at the top of the motion for an instant and slowly lower the weights back to the starting position.

Physio-Ball Twists

Step 1. Lie back on a physio-ball with your shoulders lined up with the center of the ball.

Step 2. Keeping you feet on the ground, extend your arms out (you may use a weight if necessary) toward the ceiling. Twist toward the ground until your shoulder is at the center point of the ball.

Step 3. Return to the starting position and repeat on the other side.

Medicine Ball Push Ups

Step 1. Assume a push-up position with one hand balancing on a medicine ball.

Step 2. Lower your upper body down toward the floor until the arm on the ball is at a 90-degree angle.

Step 3. Push yourself up to the starting position.

Step 4. Roll the ball to the other hand and repeat.

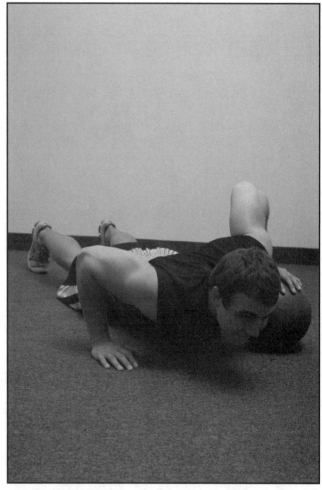

Alternating One-Legged Squat-Sits

Step 1. Sit on a bench or chair. Place one leg on the ground and stand up using only the one leg.

Step 2. Sit-down again, controlling your descent.

Step 3. Switch legs and repeat.

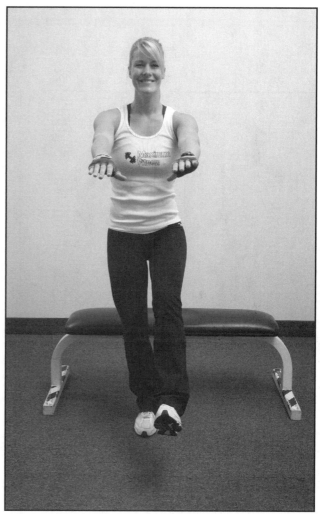

Medicine Ball Twists

Step 1. Stand up with a medicine ball in both hands extended out from your body at shoulder height.

Step 2. Twist in one direction, letting the ball travel and drop to hip level.

Step 3. Twist back to the starting position and repeat on the other side.

Pull-Ups

Step 1. Looking up at a pull-up bar, grasp it in an overhand grip with your hands slightly more than shoulder width apart. Let your body hang and completely extend your arms.

Step 2. Pull yourself up until your chin clears the bar.

Step 3. Hold for an instant and lower yourself back to down to full extension.

One-Legged Reaches

Step 1. Stand on one foot and reach both hands out and toward the floor.

Step 2. Return to the beginning position and repeat.

One-Legged Towel Squat

Step 1. Take a towel and wrap it around a pole. Hold onto the ends so that you can lean back without falling.

Step 2. Keeping your weight over your heels, squat down until your thigh is parallel to the ground.

Step 3. Hold for and instant and repeat.

Physio-Ball Push-Ups

Step 1. On an inflatable physio-ball assume a push-up position with your hands on the floor, feet on the ball.

Step 2. Keeping your body straight, push into the floor, lifting your upper body off the ground until your arms are extended.

Step 3. Hold for an instant and lower your self slowly back to the start position.

Crunches

Step 1. Lie on your back with your knees pulled up, feet on the floor, and arms folded across your chest.

Step 2. Slowly roll your shoulders toward your thighs and hold for an instant.

Step 3. Let your body roll back down to the floor and repeat.

CHAPTER 11

PRESEASON STRENGTH PROGRAM (4-6 WEEKS)

This is where the rubber meets the road. It is during the next 4-6 weeks you will push yourself to the limit. For maximum gains, 100 percent effort in the weight-room for each and every rep at each and every session. This may sound easy, but it takes discipline, dedication, and maturity to accomplish.

The strength phase of training is about just that, developing hardcore, gorilla strength. During this time our conditioning sessions will be light in order to give us maximum results in the gym. Since you will be lifting weights for close to maximum capability, it is imperative to make the period between sets count so that your body has adequate time to recover completely from the previous lift. For that reason, rest periods will be much longer than usual. Use a timer to gauge this and do not ever rush to the next set. Working with a training partner or two can aid in this, since you must rest while your other partners are performing their respective lifts.

The use of a personal listening device is also recommended. Play music prior to your lifts that will psyche you up and slower, mellowing tunes during your rest periods. Due to the heavy nature of these sessions, it is imperative that you use good form on every repetition. When possible, use a spotter or power rack/cage with crash bars to insure safety.

Performing workouts with heavy weights is extremely taxing systemically. You will need additional sleep for recovery as well as an augmented nutrition program in order to reap maximum benefits.

Always keep a log of your lifts including reps and weights used, so that you may track your progress. Done properly and with adequate recovery and nutrition, this program will help you to increase your base strength by a significant amount. It is not uncommon to see players increase their average lifts by upwards of 20 pounds per week!

THE PRESEASON STRENGTH WORKOUT

These training sessions should be performed three times a week, preferably not on consecutive days, and last no longer that one hour total, including warm up and cool down. Weights will be 85-95 percent of one rep max for 3-5 sets of 3-5 repetitions. Allow 3-5 minutes of rest between sets. All exercises should be done with free weights, specifically barbells, for maximum results. A proper and thorough warm up should be performed before each session. For purposes of illustration I will assume a Monday-Wednesday-Friday schedule, but this is up to you.

- **Monday**—Begin with squats, then bench press, finishing with hanging leg raise.
- **Wednesday**—Begin with romanian deadlifts, then weighted pull-ups. Finish with back extensions.
- **Friday**—Begin with leg press, then overhead push-press, finishing with barbell twists.

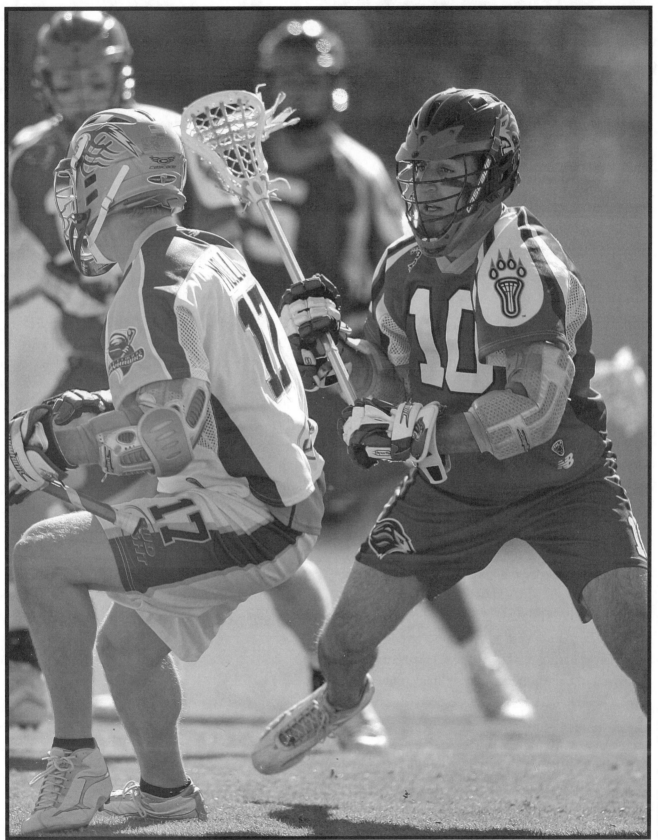

CHAPTER 12

PRESEASON EXPLOSIVE PROGRAM

This is the time when you take the strength gains achieved over the last month and begin to apply them to explosive movements. This does two things. First, it gets the neuromuscular system to adapt to the new muscle that has grown during the strength phase, and second, it begins to apply the strength you've gained to key lacrosse skills. To accomplish this, you must begin to lift weights in a ballistic fashion, using compound movements that apply speed to each lift. As always, when lifting for explosive strength, proper form is essential to make gains and prevent injury. If possible, a player should perform these lifts using barbells and rubberized bumper plates on an Olympic lifting platform.

The explosive strength gains achieved during this phase of training will translate directly into your abilities on the field. Any mass gained during the strength phase has now been capillated and neurologically wired for dynamic movement and utility. The last phase was about strength; this explosive phase is about power. Power translates into functional strength on the field. Power and explosiveness mean the ability to accelerate past an opponent, or to check them hard, or to rip a hundred-mile-an-hour shot while on the run. It is your physical ability to do these things that will give you the edge in your field play. That is why you train so hard on the gym—so things are easy on the turf!

THE EXPLOSIVE TRAINING WORKOUT

These training sessions should be performed three days a week, preferably not on consecutive days. The sessions should last no longer that one hour total, including warm-up and cool-down periods. Weights will be 70-85 percent of one rep max for 3-5 sets of 5-8 repetitions. Allow 2-3 minutes of rest between sets. All exercises should be done with free weights, specifically barbells, for maximum results. A proper and thorough warm up should be performed before each session. For purpose of illustration, I will again assume a Monday-Wednesday-Friday schedule, but this is up to you.

- **Monday**—Begin with bottom squats, then bottom bench, finishing with hanging leg raises.
- **Wednesday**—Begin with hanging cleans, then jerks, finishing with back extensions.
- **Friday**—Begin with barbell snatch, then plyo-push-ups, finish with cable twists.

REASONS TO TRAIN EXPLOSIVELY

Most athletic events involve explosive movements, quick changes of direction, and above all, power. Explosive training helps to teach your nervous system to stimulate more muscle fibers that would typically be used for the same task. For example, if you are performing a squat for a set of five reps, your nervous system will automatically choose a pace of lifting that will conserve energy and effort throughout the lift. In its endeavor to be more efficient, your body chooses to use less muscle fibers when it can pick the pace. When you ask your body to move that same weight ballistically, then the body must work much harder, and thus recruits more muscle fibers to accomplish the task. So if you train in a more traditional method, doing three sets of 10 slow, controlled reps, then you are actually programming your body to utilize its muscles slowly. But lacrosse players do not want to use their muscles slowly! The only way you can program quick muscular responses is to train explosively. Essentially, we are programming the nervous system to respond with more muscle fibers for maximum results and power transfer.

The partner to programming your muscles is training your tendons and joints to handle the added stress of explosive training. The basic equation of Power = Mass x Acceleration translates into additional demands on joints, ligaments, muscles, and tendons. Training explosively prepares the body to absorb and deal with the increased stress that you will experience while playing the game of lacrosse. Explosive training in the weight room predisposes the body to handle these incredible loads and reduces the chance of injury. It is a fact that every time you take a running stride, a shock wave equivalent to three times your body weight ripples through your body. Explosive training habituates the body to this, enhancing the ability of its connective tissue to both absorb and exert more force.

CHAPTER 13

PRESEASON BALANCE (4 WEEKS)

Now that a player has developed strength and explosiveness, the focus shifts to enhancing balance. This will allow the body to balance out its gains from the previous two phases of training by training both the dominant and non-dominant sides of the body independently and equally. This balancing of your strength gains will benefit core body strength and aid in developing true bilateral abilities in play. To accomplish this, you will begin to train exclusively with dumbbells or kettlebells and to utilize unilateral compound movements. It is important to note here that a player should always begin these workouts by training their "weak" or non-dominant side and then matching that with the "strong" or dominant side. For example, if you can snatch 40 pounds with your right hand and only 35 pounds with your left, then train both sides with 35 pounds until you can move up in weight on both sides. By training this way you will begin to balance out your functional strength while increasing dexterity and ability with your non-dominant side. Remember to check your ego at the door in this training. It is about performance training and not how much you can lift.

During this phase of training you will be using dumbbells and, if available, kettlebells for training. Kettlebells are arguably one of the most incredible tools for unilateral and functional strength development. It is a simple device that can be used very effectively in developing unique core body ability due to its unique design. Most players will use between a 20 and 40 pound kettlebell in training. Do not let the low weights fool you; a 36-pound kettlebell is infinitely more difficult to left than a dumbbell of equal weight. If kettlebells are not available or not allowed in your gym, the following exercises can also be done using standard dumbbells.

WHAT IS A KETTLEBELL?

A kettlebell, or *girya* in Russian, is a traditional cast-iron weight that looks a lot like a cannonball with a handle attached to it. It is considered by many to be the ultimate tool for extreme all-round fitness. Kettlebells tax the body to lift the weight in a complex (full body), dynamic (explosive) manner with each and every lift. The physics of the design, though simple, uses gravity, centrifugal, and centripetal forces to increase the strength curve when lifting. No other single tool does it better. In fact, many Russian athletes use kettlebells exclusively for weight training, replacing all their other gym equipment including barbells, dumbbells, belts for weighted pull-ups and dips, thick bars, lever bars, medicine balls, and grip devices.

The balancing phase of training will increase functional strength even further by taxing both sides of the body as well as the center or core. As there are no benches to push off from or barbells to grab on the playing field, this develops strength equilibrium and allows a player to apply force while supported by their body alone, whether in motion or in a non-stable platform such as when running. It is the ultimate in functional and dynamic strength. When you balance out the dominant/non-dominant sides of the body, it increases your ability to apply functional strength. In a game such as lacrosse where ambidextrousness is a huge benefit, having no "weak" side makes you constantly a threat on the field. Of course this concept of total body ability needs to be applied in the skill areas of training as well, in order for you to become completely effective as a "both ways" player.

THE BALANCE TRAINING WORKOUT

The training sessions should be performed three times a week, preferably not on consecutive days, and last no longer that 1 hour total, including warm-up and cool-down. Your weights will be 60-75 percent of one rep max for 3-5 sets of 5-8 repetitions. Allow yourself 30 seconds to 1 minute of rest between sets. All exercises should be done with free weights, specifically dumbbells or kettlebells, for maximum results. A proper and thorough warm-up should be performed before each session. For purpose of illustration, we will again assume a Monday-Wednesday-Friday schedule.

- **Monday**—Begin with the physio-ball press, then one-legged deadlift. Next, Turkish get-up, and finishing with alternate hanging leg raises.
- **Wednesday**—Begin with renegade rows, then squat press, then dumbbell/kettlebell cleans, and finally twisting back extensions.
- **Friday**—Begin with dumbbell snatch, then over head squat, then one-legged lateral raise, and finish with ball twists.

CHAPTER 14

IN-SEASON MAINTENANCE

During the season players will often be taxed to their maximum with routine practice conditioning. However, if you have been following this program, it is recommended that you continue resistance training during the season using the following bodyweight-only training program. This program will act as an active recovery stage for current in-season demands, while maintaining all gains previously achieved.

THE IN-SEASON WORKOUT

These training sessions should be performed three times a week, preferably not on consecutive days, and last no longer that 1 hour total, including warm-up and cool-down. You should performed 3-5 sets of 5-8 repetitions with 30 seconds to 1 minute of rest between sets. All exercises should be done with body weight only for maximum results. A proper and thorough warm-up should be performed before each session. For purposes of illustration we will assume a Monday–Wednesday–Friday schedule.

- **Monday**—Begin with medicine ball push-ups, then alternating one-legged squat sits, and end with medicine ball twists.
- **Wednesday**—Start with pull-ups, then one-legged reaches, finishing with back extensions.
- **Friday**—Start with towel squat, then physio-ball push-ups, and finish with crunches.

During this phase be sure to listen to your body. If you are overly fatigued from practice or game play, take a day off, or better yet, perform only one or two sets of these exercises. Remember, this is time for gains on the field and not the gym. Focus on playing the game but maintain your workout routines.

CHAPTER 15

POSTSEASON RECOVERY (4 WEEKS)

During the first month after a season players must accomplish two things. First, they must fully recover both mentally and physically from the season and make sure all their injuries are treated. Second, they must maintain a base level of fitness. It is recommended that all players take at least one full week off from any hard training before entering into these programs. Taking a break from hard training, remember, does not mean you should become a couch potato. At this time alternate physical activities such as swimming, yoga, and low-impact martial arts are great for recovery. Physiotherapy, massage, and flexibility training should be used if available.

After this week of recovery we will begin our preseason recovery training. This training is relatively light in load and intensity. It is designed to stimulate the body's recovery processes for the work to come. These training sessions may strike you as unreasonably light as a work out, but they serve the important purpose of activating the recovery response and giving the body a re-introduction to weight training postseason. Indeed, this light workout period is critical success in the future phases of the training. Though it may seem "too easy," give it the same dedication and concentration that a heavier session would demand.

THE POSTSEASON RECOVERY WORKOUT

These training sessions should be performed three times a week, preferably not on consecutive days, and last no longer that 1 hour total, including warm up and cool down. The weight used will be moderate at 50-60 percent of your 1 rep max for 3 sets of 8-10 reps. Allow a rest period of no longer that 60 seconds between sets. Exercises can be performed with free weights or machines. Be sure to use proper form to avoid injury. As before we assume a Monday-Wednesday-Friday schedule.

- **Monday**—Start with bench press, then squat, and end with lateral raises.
- **Wednesday**—Begin with rows, then romanian deadlifts, finishing with back extensions.
- **Friday**—Begin with military press, then leg press, ending with physio-ball push-ups.

CHAPTER 16

PRE-, POST-, AND IN- SEASON CONDITIONING

Lacrosse is a fast-paced game that demands superior physical conditioning. The programs in this book are designed to mimic the energy expenditures and physical demands of the game and thus produce a better-conditioned player. Many coaches are still "old school" and emphasize long runs and endurance training for a sport that does not require such ability. Though the average midfielder in a lacrosse game may run between 3-5 miles during a game, this distance covered is broken up into small, intense burst of speed and not long, slow runs. Therefore, training a player by having them perform longer runs makes no sense. As a sprinting game, with runs of 20-50 yards at most, lacrosse demands a high level of cardiovascular fitness and anaerobic endurance. Cutting, reverse of direction, and quick-explosive moves are better suited for the game, so one must condition just the same. The majority of the running done in these programs is designed to accustom the body to use the appropriate energy sources from the body when performing shorter all-out sprints while developing a high lactate threshold.

The above reenforces the methods in place here. Why train for endurance when what we are doing is explosive sprinting? In addition to the above, there have been additional studies that further the concept of power-sprint and lactate threshold training for this type of athletic endeavor.

CALCULATING YOUR MAX HEART RATE

It is important to know the intensity at which you are working to fully benefit from the different types of conditioning runs that you will be doing. The simplest way to determine your projected work-load when lifting weights is the poundage of each lift, and in conditioning it is best calculated as a percentage of maximum heart rate. To calculate your MHR do the following:

- HR percent is roughly 220 minus your age = 100% MAX HR.
- Multiply this number by the desired percent required for each run (for example 90 percent for hard sprints.
- Divide this number by 6; this is your heart rate for the percent desired over 10 seconds.
- Take your pulse by placing your index and middle fingers at your jugular (jawline) or on your wrist; count how many beats in 10 seconds.

EXAMPLE:
19-year-old: 220-19 = 201 beats per minute

201 x 0.90 = 181 beats per minute

181 ₆ 6 = 30 beats over 10 seconds

By doing this you can gauge your theoretical max efforts via your pulse rate as measure after a run or drill.

MANY athletes are confused about how long to train and, in particular, how long to run (time) for optimum fitness and conditioning. The answer lies in the body's physiological response to training and what fuel source the body taps when training at different levels of intensity and duration. Many athletes hear terms bandied about such as "lactic acid build-up" and "muscle glycogen depletion". Couple this with a true and common misunderstanding of the use of the "anaerobic versus aerobic" exercise, and you have a recipe for a host of popular myths.

Depending on the intensity and duration of an activity, your body will respond depending on what fuel source it needs to sustain such activity. The human body has a few choices when it comes to energy reserves while exercising. Each is tapped depending on the demand placed on the body itself through any physical activity. This is how energy gets to the muscles during running.

For short, explosive movements one type is used, and for longer times and distance another. Some access glycogen for fuel while others burn fat, and some use neither. High-intensity exercise of a short duration requires anaerobic sources of ATP, such as phosphocreatine. This is what fuels your legs during a 100-meter sprint or any exercise lasting less than 30 seconds. Accessing energy through anaerobic glycolysis is for high-intensity exercise of one to three minutes in duration, such as an 800-meter run. As lacrosse players rarely run more than 40 yards at a time, it is the development of the former energy source that is most effective. However, there is a limitation that goes beyond any fuel source. It is the waste product of the chemical reaction that powers our muscles, lactic acid.

When lactic acid builds up at a rate faster than it can be cleared from the muscles, the legs cramp up and the capacity to continue exercise severely diminishes. Understanding what happens to the body at different exercise intensities and distances can help you recognize and avoid the limitations of each energy system for the best effects on your training and performance. Training the body to access specific energy deposits in the body and to actively rid the body of waste product lactic acid is accomplished by training within those activity requirements. For example, if sprinting is the major event in lacrosse, then training with sprints and not long endurance runs is ideal.

The program is broken up into Postseason Recovery, Preseason (1, 2, and 3), and In-Season training. Each section is designed to work with your strength training periodization so the maximum benefits of both training areas are optimized. Warm-up and flexibility training remain the same year round as do skills and agility training.

PRESEASON CONDITIONING SESSION
(STRENGTH PHASE)   4-6 WEEKS

These sessions coincide with your strength training phase in which your joints and muscles will be taxed with heavy weight training. Therefore, we will continue to work with either a stationary bike or elliptical machine in order to give the body's joints the recovery time they need. During this period we will be asking our muscles to get bigger and stronger, so overtaxing them by performing a lot of running or high intensity cardio would be counterproductive. Nevertheless, we need to maintain a base level of aerobic and cardiovascular fitness by performing a 20-30 minute session of light resistance interval training on an exercise bike or elliptical trainer.

Mount a stationary cycle or elliptical machine. Set the machine at a resistance level that you can easily maintain for the entire period; begin pedalling/walking for 5 minutes and then adjust the resistance up a level or two for 5 minutes. Return to your original resistance setting and begin intervals. Ride at the current setting for 1 minute, and then keeping the machine at this same resistance level, increase your pace. Pedal/step as fast as you can at this resistance level for 30 seconds, then return to your original level and repeat: 1 minute resting rate, 30 seconds sprint for 4-6 cycles. Return to your original pace for 5 minutes. This should be performed on off-days from your strength training days in order to give maximum recovery. Perform these sessions 3 times/week.

PRESEASON CONDITIONING SESSION
(EXPLOSIVE)   4-6 WEEKS

Interval Runs and Jump Rope
It is during this time that we will be concentrating on explosive strength in the weightroom and full body conditioning at the track. Jumping rope is one of the best cardiovascular exercises there is. It increases fitness while developing agility and a "lightness of foot." Add rope sessions to the end of your explosive training in the gym begin by jumping for 1 minute nonstop with a 1-minute rest in between. Build up to 3-5 rounds of 1-minute jumping. On the off-days from the gym, go to the track and engage in interval runs. Perform a light warm-up lap then sprint the straightaways at 75 percent of your full speed capacity/maximum heart rate, and walk the turns. Begin with 1 mile (four laps on most tracks) and build up to 2-3 miles by adding an additional lap each week of this phase of training.

PRESEASON CONDITIONING
(BALANCE)   4-6 WEEKS
During the balance phase we will begin to really pour it on with our running and conditioning. The following workouts should be performed each once a week on the off-days of your weightroom training. Perform each one of the following routines once a week on your off-days from the gym.

Hill Sprints
Find a nice 20-40 yard hill. Begin at the base of the hill and sprint up a fast as possible. Be sure to breathe and keep your arms pumping. Walk back down the hill and wait 30 seconds, then sprint again. Perform 5-10 sprints.

Medicine Ball Runs
At a field, throw a 6-12 pound medicine ball using any method that allows you to get a decent throw, then sprint after the ball and throw again from one end of the field to the next. Rest 30 seconds and then do another length of the field run. Repeat 5-10 runs.

220's
Run one quarter of a lap of the track as fast as you can, then walk or jog the remaining three quarters of the track, then sprint again. Repeat 5-10 times.

THE LACROSSE TRAINING BIBLE

IN-SEASON CONDITIONING VARIABLES

The program uses a combination of team relays, interactive sprint drills, and interval runs to produce superior athletic performance while building teamwork. Beyond developing a high level of strength and fitness, conditioning programs should help teams build cooperation and camaraderie. To that end, intersquad competitions and relays are often used. Each relay will task the team with a physical challenge as well as a cooperative challenge that can only be overcome by teamwork and synergy. This type of friendly competition instills a competitive spirit and establishes a culture of merit in which hard work and team effort translate into success, and less than stellar team performance brings tough consequences, just as in a game.

Conditioning should take place at the end of practice. Duration of the training should be 20-30 minutes in length. The goal is intensity and maximum output, not movement for movement's sake. Each day should have a slightly different emphasis in order to give players the opportunity to recover and to keep the sessions from becoming too tedious. The basic schedule breaks up the workouts to ensure maximum benefit while allowing players to recover, so one day will contain more sprints while another will have more anaerobic conditioning.

The split breaks down into team relays which task players to work together to complete a physically demanding task that combines both strength and conditioning components, more traditional sprints, interval runs, and 220-yard lactate threshold runs, as well as whole body anaerobic/cardio hybrid workouts. Team relays can be made quite difficult but fun to perform.

Little Bear Runs

Little Bear runs are similar to the traditional "Indian runs" in that the team lines up and begins moving as one in a bear crawl, which is to say on all fours. The player at the end of the line then gets up and sprints to the beginning of the line where he drops down and continues the crawl. A 100-yard or half lap relay doing this activity is an incredible strength and conditioning workout that incorporates the entire body.

Team Push-Ups

The team push-up is a relay race in which each team member begins in a push-up position with his feet hooked over the shoulders of the man behind him. On the "go" command, the entire team must perform a push-up. As they are linked together, each player must work together to accomplish this difficult task. When one push-up is completed the last person in the chain then sprints to the front and they perform another team push-up. It may sound simple, but it is quite difficult physically and takes coordination and communication on the part of the team to be able to complete the race. It works the upper body and core while providing a cardio workout via the sprints. This should be done over a 20-50 yard space. Once the last person in the chain crosses the finish line, the entire team must sprint back to the starting point.

Once again team members line up in file, and the player at the end of the line must pick up the next man in a fireman's carry and race to the front of the line. This continues until the entire team has covered the designated route, typically 50 yards. Once the last man is over the line the entire team must sprint back to the starting point.

Cage Races

Each team picks up a lacrosse goal, also known as a cage, and while holding it off the ground must cover a set distance without dropping it. Most collegiate goals weigh over 100 pounds, so this is not as easy as it may sound, especially if the team must hold it over their heads while running 200 yards.

No matter which team conditioning exercise you choose, it is important that performance be rewarded and penalties assessed for failure. Regardless of who the winner is there should be additional conditioning in the form of calisthenics to complete the workout and provide some active recovery. This motivates the team to work hard in order to win and reflects the reality of consequence for lack of performance. Winners will perform a reduced number of calisthenics and the losers will get the maximum number. It pays to be a winner!

More traditional conditioning methods, such as interval runs, are also used. This allows players to a rest day from upper body conditioning. If a track is available, then one can perform a mile or so of sprint/jogs in which players jog or walk for 1 minute and sprint for a 30 second interval. Another variation on this is the traditional "Indian run" in which players form a line and begin to jog. The last player in line sprints to the front of the line and resumes jogging. This is done nonstop for up to 30 minutes.

The next training day should once again combine upper body and cardio training that simulates the expenditures of actual play. D-sprints do just that. This is a 25-yard sprint to the line where push-ups and sit-ups are performed before sprinting back. This simulates a sprint to the hole, playing defense using your upper body, and a sprint back after shot/clear or a ground ball. The number of push-ups and sit-ups is variable depending on the level of fitness off the players.

For an ultimate challenge use a pyramid system in which the number of push-ups and sit-ups increases each repetition until someone cannot perform them, after which you subtract one for each successive repetition until we reach zero. The

goal is a sprint, push-up/sit-up, sprint pyramid that goes to 10 and back down: 2-4-6-8-10-8-6-4-2. A session like this yields eighteen 25-yard sprints and 50 push-ups and sit-ups.

Lastly, some form of lactate threshold training needs to be in place to address this aspect of conditioning. One of the most effective is 220s or quarter lap runs. This pushes the lactate threshold in each player to the max. Have players begin by walking the endline. When they reach the first corner of the field have them sprint to the midfield line, turning the corner and crossing the field. When they reach the far end of the field have them slow to a jog until the endline where they begin to walk. Perform 6-10 of these at maximum intensity.

As can be seen, this type of program strives to develop both strength and conditioning in players. The variations on training serve to balance out the program and help to reduce injury from overuse. It also helps to keep players from becoming too bored, a problem that is seen often in youth lacrosse programs.

For light or pregame days, team skill-based games are played such as Ultimate Lacrosse, which is Ultimate Frisbee using lacrosse balls and sticks. This game forces players to work on their off-ball movement and throwing and catching skills, without the pressure of physical play and checking. It's a great workout and just plain fun.

Another variation is All-Touch in which each team must complete a pass to every member of the team without dropping the ball to score a point. You can even play full-field Capture the Flag. Harking back to the true root of the game, this version goes until one team gets their lacrosse ball into the other team's goal. These are fun, creative ways in which to keep players loose and conditioned while developing game based skills. Because these drills do not contain hard checks or contact, it is also a great opportunity for the coaching staff to participate.

An example of a week-long program for the high school varsity level is as follows:

Day 1- Team push-up relay
Day 2- Interval training
Day 3- D-sprints
Day 4- Quarter laps
Day 5- Little Bear relay

POSTSEASON RECOVERY

The best thing you can do during the postseason is some light cardio training. Perform a 20-30 minute moderate level session on the stationary or elliptical machine. Perform this type of conditioning workout along with your postseason recovery strength-training sessions. For best results, combine the two into a 1-hour session three times a week. On the off-days perform any low-impact physical activity; swimming is highly recommended as well as yoga or a soft form of martial arts, such as tai chi. Remember this period is about recovering from the season and priming the body for the upcoming strength and conditioning sessions that are to come.

ULTIMATE LAX

One of the most fun and invigorating games you can play for lacrosse conditioning and skills development is Ultimate Lax, a variation on the internationally played game of Ultimate Frisbee. The field is divided up into two halves with "end zones" designated at each end. Players must move and pass the ball to one another while progressing up the field in an attempt to score by entering the end zone with possession of the ball. The trick is that no player can run with the ball. Once caught, a player can take no more than three steps to stop themselves, then basketball-like rules apply allowing players a one-foot pivot only. If the ball is dropped, knocked down, or intercepted by an opposing player, then possession goes to the other team. This game takes a lot of off-ball movement, creativity, and stick skills. It is also a great way to observe team dynamics and see who the leaders on the field will be. A 30-minute game of Ultimate Lax is a great workout and great fun.

CHAPTER 17

FLEXIBILITY TRAINING

Flexibility is a key factor in overall physical fitness. Limber muscles are more efficient in their movements, and they are less prone to injury. There are many methods of flexibility training, all of which work in some capacity or another. For the lacrosse player, flexibility is part of recovery from hard training as well as a method of injury avoidance. Note here that the term "stretching" is not being used. There are studies that show the "old school" stretching may not only be less than effective for some athletes, it may even help to cause injuries. Because of these findings and from the author's experience we will use the term "movements" in lieu of "stretching." This difference is more than just semantics; it reflects the methodology in which specific movements are used to cool down the muscle groups after intense training. The majority of the movements described are mirror images of our warm ups and are designed to provide flexibility training via controlled dynamic movements and not static stretches. The movements designated here are just samples of the cool-down exercises a player can use. The important issue is not what movements are used use, but how they are applied.

The body has a natural response to stretching sometimes called a "flinch" response that tightens any muscle being stretched beyond its comfort zone. It is the body's natural method of protection. In order that we do not work against this response it is important to use a different method of flexibility training so that we help to overcome this protection mechanism and allow the muscles to relax, so we can insure an increase in functional flexibility without injury. To do this we will perform a movement briefly, releasing the end position after 2-3 seconds, and then repeating it. Keep relaxed and continue breathing when performing any movement. Also, lightly flex the antagonistic muscle group to help relax the muscle being used. For example, while in a movement to increase flexibility of the hamstring, lightly flex the quad of that same leg. This will help the body to relax the muscle even more. On the last rep of each movement, breathe out, flex the antagonistic muscle, and hold the position while continuing to breathe for as long as is comfortable.

Many players skimp on this aspect of training due to its lack of dynamism. Some feel it is too boring and tedious, but the benefit to the player is immeasurable. Many coaches do not allow adequate time for postpractice flexibility training due to time constraints. It is important to allow adequate time in a practice session for this. It will keep your players loose and injury free.

It is recommended that coaches use this time to work with players and to keep players focused on the task at hand. No discussion of team dynamics, plays, or anything else should take place that induces a stress response. Players need to be relaxed, and so does the coach. Plus, this instills the importance to the posttraining flexibility/cool-down period. If physically possible, a coach should participate in warm-up drills, conditioning, and flexibility training. This builds camaraderie and true team spirit. If there is an equipment manager or assistant coaches, they too should participate.

The following program is designed to be more dynamic, enjoyable, and time efficient by combining movements in a yoga-like flow that keeps the player moving. In an effort to keep this aspect of our training fun and effective, this program should be done nonstop, moving from one movement to the next applying a 5 rep hold of 2-3 seconds with a longer 10-second hold on the fifth rep. Then move onto the next one. It should take no more that 5-10 minutes to complete.

© Taufan Tjioe

Sometimes the game—even in scrimmages—can be rough.

Reach Back/Bend Forward

Step 1. Stand with your feet shoulder width apart.

Step 2. Reach up and back with your arms toward the sky and slightly backwards

Step 3. Hold for 2-3 seconds.

Step 4. Bend forward toward the ground and wrap your arms around your upper thighs.

Step 5. Squeeze for 2-3 seconds.

Step 6. Return to you starting position.

Repeat for 5 reps holding for up to 10 seconds on the last rep.

Side Bends

Step 1. Raise your hands high over your head.

Step 2. Bend to one side.

Step 3. Hold that position for 2-3 seconds

Step 4. Return to the start position.

Step 5. Perform the same movement to the opposite side.

Repeat for 5 reps holding for 10 seconds on the last rep.

Arm Rotations

Step 1. Stand upright and bring your arms out to the side at shoulder height with your palms facing up.

Step 2. Rotate your palms forward as far as comfortable, turning the back of your hand toward the ground.

Step 3. Hold that position for 2-3 seconds.

Step 4. Rotate backwards past the start position as far as comfortable, turning your palms toward the ground.

Step 5. Hold that position for 2-3 seconds.

Repeat for 5 reps holding for up to 10 seconds on the last rep.

The Hulk

Step 1. Stand upright and reach both arms around your chest, as if to hug yourself.

Step 2. Pull the arms together, flex your chest and abs, and allow the muscles of the upper back to stretch.

Step 3. Hold that position for 2-3 seconds.

Step 4. Open your arms up and pull back, flexing the muscles of the upper back and arms to allow for a stretch of the chest.

Step 5. Hold that position for 2-3 seconds.

Step 6. Return to start position.

Repeat for 5 reps holding for up to 10 seconds on the last rep.

Drop and Push

Step 1. Assume a push-up position.

Step 2. While keeping your arms extended and locked, drop your hips toward the floor and pull your head back, nose to the sky.

Step 3. Hold that position for 2-3 seconds.

Step 4. Drop your head back to the ground and while keeping your legs straight, push your buttocks up into the air forming an upside-down V with your body.

Step 5. Hold that position for 2-3 seconds.

Repeat for 5 reps holding for up to 10 seconds on the last rep.

Scorpions

Step 1. Lie flat on your belly with your arms extended out 90 degrees to your body.

Step 2. While keeping your arms and upper body on the ground, rotate your foot up and toward the opposite hand, letting your hips off the ground if necessary.

Step 3. Hold that position for 2-3 seconds.

Step 4. Return to the start position.

Step 5. Perform the same movement on the other side.

Repeat for 5 reps holding for up to 10 seconds on the last rep.

The Cat

Step 1. Begin on all fours.

Step 2. Push your midback up to the sky, rounding your back as much as possible.

Step 3. Hold for that position for 2-3 seconds.

Step 4. Allow your abdomen to drop back down toward the floor and push.

Step 5. Hold for that position for 2-3 seconds.

Repeat for 5 reps holding for up to 10 seconds on the last rep.

Sumo Squat

Step 1. Squat down with your toes pointed out at 45 degrees.

Step 2. Place your elbows inside your thighs.

Step 3. Let your buttocks hang down and push your inner thighs outward with your elbows.

Step 4. Hold for that position for 2-3 seconds.

Step 5. Extend your legs keeping your hands on the floor.

Repeat for 5 reps holding for up to 10 seconds on the last rep.

Hamstring Squat

Step 1. From the Sumo squat position, extend one of your legs out to your side keeping the toe pointed to the sky.

Step 2. Turn your upper body toward your extended foot and push your nose out and over your thigh.

Step 3. Hold for that position for 2-3 seconds.

Step 4. Return to start position.

Step 5. Perform the same on the other leg.

Repeat for 5 reps holding for up to 10 seconds on the last rep.

Buddha Squats

Step 1. Begin standing.

Step 2. Cross one leg over the thigh of other leg.

Step 3. Squat down, keeping the opposite leg crossed over you squatting leg.

Step 4. Hold that position for 2-3 seconds.

Step 5. Return to start position.

Step 6. Switch legs and repeat on the opposite side.

Repeat for 5 reps holding for up to 10 seconds on the last rep.

Californian

Step 1. Lie flat on your back and breath deeply and allow all your muscles to go completely limp.

Step 2. Hold for 10-30 seconds or until you fall asleep.

PART III

•••

THE BASIC SKILLS OF LACROSSE

Training your body to be the most athletic it can be is the basis for lacrosse performance on the field. But in lacrosse, athletic ability is just the beginning. A highly developed set of skills is also necessary. Fielding ground balls, throwing, catching, dodging, and shooting are all fundamental skills of the game. This section of the book will take you through each skill step-by-step and offer breakdowns of each skill for novice players as well as drills for every level of play.

Lacrosse is a very athletic event; it necessitates speed, balance, power, and skill. Like most sports played using man-to man match-ups, it is important to stay balanced and loose so that you can react quickly to any opportunity on the field. To do this you need to begin with the basic dynamic positioning that will allow you maximum flexibility in your movement on the field. In lacrosse that position is the dynamic ready position. The dynamic ready position is a way of prepositioning your body so that you are prepared to throw, catch, dodge, or scoop a ground ball. It is a simple stance in which you keep our body positioned for maximum stick protection. To assume the dynamic ready position, stand facing your partner with your legs at shoulder width. Take a slight step forward placing with one foot (left foot if right-handed, right foot if left-handed). This foot position is imperative because it will give you balance and force your upper body to turn slightly so that you get maximum protection for your stick. Being bipedal, upright creatures, a human must slightly offset the feet in order to achieve both lateral and linear stability. By placing our feet this way we are then prepared to move in any direction. Keeping your weight balanced equally on each foot, bend your knees slightly with your weight more on the balls of your feet. This keeps the legs primed and ready to go as well as maintaining balance.

With your base now well established, you will find that your body will be slightly offset to your partner as well, with the front shoulder pointing towards him. This is a perfect position for the upper body to receive a pass or to throw. Keeping your head up and eyes open. Hold your stick vertically and bring the head of the stick to a position slightly forward of your head, right off of the brow line. This places the stick in a position to receive a pass by giving you a good open target. It also allows for a receiving cushion in order to properly catch the ball. Most importantly, it places you in a position to throw and move quickly. Check yourself in a mirror if need be.

Now you are ready to play!

CHAPTER 18

CRADLING: THREE TECHNIQUES TO MASTER

Cradling is like dribbling in basketball. Its purpose is to control the ball while prepositioning it in the belly of the pocket for a shot or a pass. Proper cradling allows you to control the ball in the stick while running, dodging, shooting, and throwing. It is one of the essential skills needed to play the game.

There are two basic ways of cradling, as we will explain, and there is also a prethrow or transition cradle. The prethrow cradle allows you to transition from controlling the ball in the stick to being able to throw or shoot the ball. Mastering these three cradling techniques builds the base that will allow you to go beyond anything novices can imagine. Skills such as cradling with your stick upside down while flying through the air and performing other spectacular moves will become natural to you. The greatest players in the game perform gravity-defying maneuvers that look more like magic tricks than sport moves.

American field players usually prefer a two-handed method of cradling when away from a defender and a one-handed cradle when going one-on-one to the goal. But this rule is not set in stone. Many field players will switch from one method or the other as play dictates.

The Canadian box lacrosse players rarely if ever use a one-handed cradle. They prefer to keep two hands on the stick and employ a "power cradle." In a "power cradle" the bottom hand is pressed tightly against the body near the hip and the top hand cradles with great force and rapidity.

Many or even most indoor players also favor a different style of cradling. They use only one side, right or left, and rarely switch hands, whatever their position on the field. Indeed, it is common in the indoor game to see a right-handed player drive to the left and simply hold the stick out with their bottom hand, carrying the ball *sans* cradle.

Most outdoor American players strive to have equal ability with both hands, and this ambidextrous style is the one we will emphasize. But whichever version of the sport you play, good cradling is a must. Proper cradling technique is a key to success on the field or in the box.

CRADLING DRILLS

Cradling is a basic skill that can be practiced anytime, anywhere. No partner is needed, no wall, and no equipment except for a stick and ball. It is the skill that is used most often by a player and, like dribbling in basketball, is a skill that makes or breaks your game. There are, as we said, two basic ways to cradle: one-handed and two-handed. There is also a prethrow/shoot cradle. We will begin with the one-handed cradle.

The One-Handed Cradle

The one-handed cradle is used when a player is being pressured by a defender and must give maximum protection to the stick so that it cannot be checked and the ball dislodged. By cradling with one hand off the stick, an offensive player can place his body and off-hand arm between the defender. The stick is thus well protected from checks. Though this method of cradling gives protection from checks, it does not allow a player to throw or shoot without first placing both hands on the stick.

In advanced applications, the one-handed cradle is combined with dodges and cuts that allow an offensive player to move aggressively against a defender while keeping the ball in his stick. It is imperative to have this sort of skill if you want to be an offensive threat on the field. Though typically taught as the more advanced skill, one-handed cradling is actually much easier to learn than two-handed cradling. Mastering the one-handed cradle is the basis for all other cradling methods and should therefore be taught first as part of the "part/whole" method of skill development. To perform a one-handed cradle:

Step 1. Assume the ready position: stick up, feet offset, chest out, knees bent, and head up.

Step 2. Grasp the shaft of the stick just below the base of the head as if holding a hammer or an ice cream cone. Make sure that the open face of the stick is facing your chest.

Step 3. While keeping the stick vertical to the ground, rotate the wrist forward toward your opposite shoulder. Allow the head of the stick to turn inward toward your body.

Step 4. Once the head has been rotated so that you can see the back of the stick, reverse the direction and rotate the head back so that the face of the stick is back to the starting position. Use a waving motion that keeps your elbow close to the body.

Remember that it is mainly a movement of the wrist and forearm that moves the head of the stick in an arc back and forth while centrifugal force keeps the ball pressed into the mesh. Perform this drill using first your dominant hand, then your nondominant hand.

The One-Handed Cradle

Switching Hands

The goal in the one-hand drills is to be able to cradle with both hands equally well. When you can do this, the next step is to begin switching hands while cradling.

Step 1. Bring the head of the stick to the center of your body right in front of your face.

Step 2. While centering the stick, bring your off-hand to the stick and grasp the stick as far up the shaft as possible just under the cradling hand.

Step 3. Let go of the stick with your cradling hand and allow the stick to travel to the opposite side of your body. Cradle with the hand that just grabbed on.

This basic skill of one-handed cradling and the ability to switch hands is paramount to learning the two-handed cradling technique. Practice this every day striving for 100 repetitions of cradle/switch/ cradle per day. This will help to develop proper form and muscle memory. Once the one-handed cradle is mastered, then the two-handed can be learned with ease.

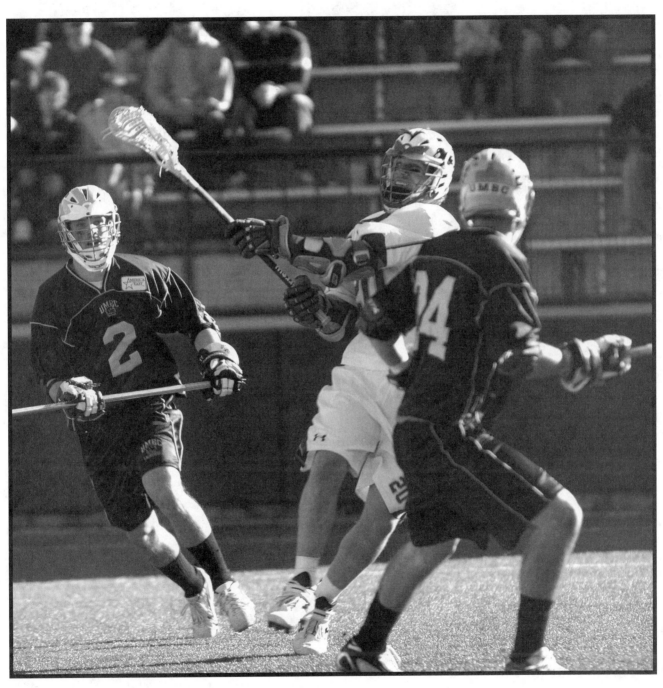

© Dugald Munro

The Two-Handed Cradle

The two-handed cradle is a very important skill every lacrosse player must master. No matter your position on the lacrosse field, everybody needs to be able to cradle with two hands. It is essential when moving with the ball. Two-handed cradling allows you to play with both hands on the stick, giving you the ability to throw, catch, or shoot while on the move. In fact, many players become so adept at two-handed cradling that they rarely if ever use the one-handed method.

Step 1. Place your off-hand at the butt-end of your shaft. Make the "OKAY" sign with your fingers forming a hole for the end of the stick to sit. The bottom hand should be placed at the center of your body at hip level. This bottom hand does nothing but loosely hold the butt-end of the stick. What it does is cause the stick to lean toward the top-hand side a bit. Let it.

Step 2. Now begin performing a one-handed cradle with your top hand. Let the bottom end of the stick rotate in your bottom hand. Perform this both left-and right-handed.

Step 3. When that is comfortable, add a switch of hands. To do this, bring the stick to your face just as with the one-handed switch. Slide your bottom hand up to your top hand. Let go of the top hand and bring it down to the bottom of the stick.

Perform this everyday, striving for 100 repetitions of cradle/switch/cradle per day.

The Two-Handed Cradle

Once the two basic cradles are comfortable, begin changing the position of your stick as you hold the cradle. For example, cradle in front of your body, then to your top-hand side, then to your bottom-hand side by moving both your arms and rotating your body. Learn to move your upper body while continuing to cradle. Imagine defenders coming at you from different directions. Use your body as a shield while keeping your cradling steady and controlled. Once this is beginning to feel comfortable, begin to perform these drills while walking, then jogging, and finally at sprinting speed. Eventually you will be cradling while dodging defenders and cutting to the goal at full speed, all the while staying in complete control of the ball.

The Prethrow or Transition Cradle

The transition or prethrow cradle is an often-overlooked skill. The positioning of the top hand while cradling to protect the ball is different that the positioning of the top hand on preparation for throwing the ball. Since every lacrosse player needs to move the ball quickly by passing, the transition move must be part of his repertoire. When in prethrow mode, a player changes the position of the top hand from a hammer grip to a tennis grip. This transition or change in grip is one that gives many novice lacrosse players trouble and is unfortunately ignored by most coaches.

Step 1. Begin with a two-handed cradle.

Step 2. On the rearward movement of the cradle, grip the stick with your bottom hand.

Step 3. Slide the stick upward using your bottom hand while changing the grip of our top hand from a hammer to a tennis grip (see illustration).

This places your stick and hand in a position that is optimal for throwing. This transition move should be added to your cradling practice on both left and right sides. Aim for 100 repetitions per day.

Transition Drill

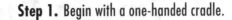

Now that the mechanics of the transition grip are clear, a player must practice it in different situations. Often a player may be moving up the field, cradling with two hands, only to be challenged by an aggressive defender who forces a transition to a one-handed cradle. Sometimes at this point the player decides to pass the ball instead of going one-on-one with this defender. He must therefore transition instantly from carrying the ball in a two-handed cradle to a prethrow cradle. There are many variations on this move to practice.

The transition drill that follows is just one of many you may do. It may be helpful to try this drill in front of a mirror so that you can watch your form and see what you are doing. Remember, the goal is perfect muscle memory on both sides so that we can become the best player we can be.

Step 1. Begin with a one-handed cradle.

Step 2. Add the bottom hand and perform a two-handed cradle for a couple reps.

Step 3. For two cradles then transition to a two-handed cradle for two repetitions, then transition to a prethrow cradle for two repetitions, then back to a normal two-handed cradle for two repetitions, and back to a one-handed cradle for two repetitions. Then switch to the other side and do the same. The goal is to be able to move from one to two to prethrow smoothly and without dropping the ball.

CHAPTER 19

FIELDING GROUND BALLS

One of the most important skills of the game is being able to pick up a ball that is on the ground. Every lacrosse player must learn to pick up a ground ball very quickly and get control of it in his stick. Indeed, the game starts at a face off where the ball is placed on the ground. The ability of a player to aggressively pick up a ground ball and get it moving through the air or by running with it in his stick is crucial to winning games. So important is this skill with ground balls that many college players are recruited based on this statistic alone. Whichever team can pick up the most ground balls usually controls and wins the game.

Both American field and Canadian box lacrosse have their distinct methods of picking up grounders. On the field a ball is usually picked up with a two-handed method as described in this chapter; in the box via a quick one-handed scoop or a neat trick called an "Indian pick-up." Due to the rapid development of high-tech playing surfaces, we are seeing less grass on fields and more artificial turf. This advance in the game is pushing ground ball techniques further toward the box camp, in which one needs less effort to pick up a ball. Nevertheless, both Canadian and American coaches emphasize the same three basics: get low, stay low, and scoop through. Practice this way and you will become the ground ball king of your team, mastering of one of the most important skills in the game.

Two-handed

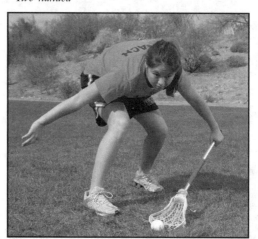

One-handed

The ability to pick up a ground ball in a small basket on the end of a stick is not a natural thing. With a pack of wild defensemen on your heels, it can be downright scary. But you must do it! Being able to do it consistently and well guarantees a player a starting position in just about any team at

any level. The keys to good ground ball handling are body orientation, body position (getting down low), and stick position. Putting all three together will give you great skill at the ground ball game.

Ideally, as a player approaches a ground ball, he begins to lower his body and stick several yards before he encounters the ball. With both body and stick properly positioned, a player continues to run towards the ground ball. He allows the head of the stick to pass under the ball, which is captured by the momentum of his running body and the scooping motion of his stick. Once the ball is in

the stick, the player begins to stand up. He brings the head of the stick up to his face or chest, thereby protecting the stick from being checked. Depending on the situation, a player will continue running to an open portion of the field or immediately pass it off to a teammate.

The complete capturing motion is sometimes compared to a bird swooping down to pick up prey. It is a skill that requires intensive practice and the perfection of the three basic subskills. It all starts with ball orientation.

Ball Orientation

Ball orientation is the primary factor for success in picking up ground balls. It is the ability to judge your distance from the ball on the ground while you are moving toward it. This may seem obvious, but none of us are born with a 3-6 foot stick in our hands, so it is important that a player begin by becoming adept at relating to the ball this way. People are used to picking something off the ground by walking up to it, usually so that it is right at our feet, then bending down and picking it up with our hands. If a player walks or runs right up to the ball with stick in hand, it is virtually impossible to pick up. The ball has no way of leaping up into the head of the stick, and the player has no way of scooping the ball up at this distance. So the first task is to learn to get a proper line on a ground ball at least 3-5 yards before the actual location of the ball. Developing this ability will allow a player with good ground ball form to pick up any ball on the ground at a dead run.

Pick-Up Stick Drill

Step 1. Place a ball on the ground and then lay a lacrosse stick in front of it with the head of the stick a few inches from the ball itself.

Step 2. Now have the player walk quickly up to the stick, bending down and grapping it with both hands.

Step 3. As the player continues to move forward have him stay low and try to scoop up the ball.

This drill begins to orient the player to a ground ball by using their stick and not their hands. The distance is set via the placement of the stick. The player is forced to get low in order to pick up the stick, and he learns the movement of scooping that is body dependent rather than just standing up straight and poking down at a ball with their stick, a common mistake for beginning players. Once a player develops the ability to orient to the ball on the ground while moving, increase the speed at which they approach the drill. Then eventually allow them to begin with the stick in their hands. If the initial practice has gone well, then they will quickly be able to orient to the ball using their stick.

Body Position

Once a player begins to develop the ability to orient to the ball on the ground, positioning his body becomes the issue. In order to insure success at ground balls a player must prepositioning his body so that he will be able to pick up the ground ball while maintaining his speed, protecting his stick, and avoiding checks from an opposing player. The position universally best suited for ground balls is the low crouch.

Many coaches have gone hoarse admonishing players to "get low" when going after ground balls. Getting your body low helps to provide stability, protection, and getting the proper angle on the ball you want to scoop. Many players do not get low enough and therefore expose themselves to checks from a more aggressively positioned player. One drill to develop this ability is the under the bridge drill.

Under the Bridge Drill

This is a fun drill that forces players to "get low" when going after a ground ball. Note that this drill should be performed with helmet on to avoid injuries.

Step 1. Place a ball on the ground and have a coach or player stand next to the ball with a stick extended at bellybutton level over the ball.

Step 2. Now have another player run toward the ground ball, "get low" enough to duck under the extended stick, and scoop through the ball.

Step 3. Try to get control of the ball immediately so you are ready to pass it.

This drill drives home the point and neurologically programs a player to bend low for a ground ball. When this drill becomes second nature, the coach or player holding the barrier stick may add a small check to the back hand of the scoping player. This is to help the player habituate himself to the possibility of a check and to drill proper body positioning in order to prevent this.

Stick Position and the Cross-body Scoop

The last part of successful ground-balling is the position of the stick while scooping. It is important that your top hand is as close to the head of the stick as possible to ensure proper pick up and control of the ball once scooped. An excellent drill to develop this is the cross-body one-handed scoop.

Step 1. Place a ball on the ground and have players scoop the ball on the run.

Step 2. While holding the stick with their top hand across their body have them drop down and pick up the ground ball.

This drill forces players to keep their top hand high near the head of the stick and to make sure that the stick head gets low and under the ball. This may be a difficult drill to master, but once you put into muscle memory it will guarantee great ground ball positioning.

Putting the Ground Ball Skills Together

We must learn each of these ground ball skills as a separate skill, but it is the ability to combine them that makes a solid ground ball player. Drill each part separately as part of an overall skill workout, but then start to combine them in general practices. A player's goal is to never miss an open ground ball while playing and practicing lacrosse. Indeed, it is an even greater goal to never miss a ground ball while being challenged by other players. This is a skill that must be developed, and when perfected will make you a great player. Besides picking up ground balls that are stationary a player needs to practice picking up ground balls that are moving as well. As players skills develop, one should begin fielding ground balls that are moving toward the player as well as away and in every direction. Add this kind of multidirectional ground ball training to your basic drills.

This is an advanced topic, but let me conclude with a few words about fielding moving balls. Fielding a ground ball coming to you is very much like stopping a grounder in baseball. One must choke up on the stick to create a "glove" with the head of the stick while bending low to allow the ball to roll into the stick. In addition to getting down on the ball, getting your body behind the stick will help to prevent missed ground balls, for your body will act like a back stop for any ball missed. This can be performed with a low crouch, and in extreme cases, from your knees. This same method of getting a ground ball coming towards you can also be used for fielding passes that have bounced short of you. Again the basics remain: ball orientation, stick body position, and stick position. Practice this often and you will be come a ground ball hog.

CHAPTER 20

CATCHING

Catching a lacrosse ball is a combination of science and art. The science is based on simple physics and geometry, the art on style and grace of motion. Grabbing a small ball moving at speeds of more than 70 miles an hour with a small basket is a challenge, but one that can be overcome with the mastery of a few skills. One of the biggest frustrations coaches have is seeing players whose athletic talents far surpass their current stick skills. These players, unfortunately, have not received quality instruction in such basic movements as catching. This happens, more often than not, in the rush to "get the skill down" so that the player is ready to take the field in a game. The challenge all coaches and players have is to have the patience to learn the basics perfectly. Then and only then can a player develop to his full potential.

Both indoor and outdoor players share a common secret for catching the ball. This is lacrosse called "soft hands." What this term refers to is the player's ability to give with and cushion a ball entering the head of the stick. Proper cushioning will allow you to catch any ball thrown, no matter how fast. It also gives you the ability to immediately control the ball in the stick from first contact.

No additional compensating movement is needed, no cradling or slapping at the ball, just a nice cushioning catch caused by the player's ability to "give with the ball" (as if catching an egg).

This remarkable skill comes from the same cushioning movement that is needed when controlling a hockey puck with a stick. This movement requires the use of the bottom hand as a guide while the top hand acts almost exclusively as a shock absorber. Unfortunately, most American players have never played hockey or a sport that necessitates this soft-handed skill, so they tend to lack this ability. The closest analogous movement perhaps comes from our nation's pastime, baseball, but baseball does not require "soft hands" catching. Most catches in baseball also occur with the opposite hand that you throw with. Just the opposite is true in lacrosse, so many American players who come to lacrosse have to learn to catch in a way that is completely foreign to them. Some coaches try to teach catching by using the head of the stick like a baseball mitt, but this almost invariably fails. All of this puts American players at a slight disadvantage when they start to learn this crucial skill. However, all hope is not lost.

The methods and drills covered in this book combine both the box bottom-hand and the American top-hand methods of catching. The combination of these approaches produces superior catching, allowing a player to catch at any angle and to control the ball no mater how hard it is thrown. To facilitate learning, it is best to have a skilled player or coach partner with a novice player. The partner will throw the lacrosse balls to the player with their hands. The partner uses hands, not a lacrosse stick, to insure proper placement of the ball in the learning drills. One of the challenges in teaching lacrosse is to insure consistently good throws in training. A bad throw will almost never result in a good catch. Make sure you provide an accurate throw so that catching may be learned properly.

MATT BROWN'S TIPS FOR CATCHING

The key to catching the ball is to focus in on the ball until it hits your basket. I feel that using your bottom hand on the stick (If you're right-handed it would be your left hand and if you're left-handed it would be your right hand) makes it easier to locate passes that are outside of the box (the target area around your shoulders). Using your bottom hand as a control allows you to make catches that are farther away from your body and helps to strengthen your off hand.

When I first learned to catch I was taught to keep my top hand on the stick open, forcing me to use my bottom hand. A big mistake that young players make is that they punch at the ball with their top hand. It is a lot harder to catch the ball if you punch at it. What I tell my players is to think of the stick as a pillow. Imagine a ball hitting a soft pillow; the pillow cushions the ball, not making much or any sound at all. That is how you should catch. Keep your eyes open, watch it come into your stick, and cushion the ball.

Top-Hand Catching

Our nervous system must learn to catch a thrown ball not with our hands but with our sticks. This is typically something totally alien to novice players, and it is difficult enough to accomplish while standing still, much less while moving at speed. Therefore, as teachers and coaches, we should break the catching movement up into component parts. Separately learned components help players become comfortable with their new reference point. The best way is probably to begin with a one-handed technique that allows the player to use their dominant hand to control the placement of the head in reference to the moving ball. This method is typically easier to learn, since we begin with the hand held high on the stick, and, if needed, even grasp the bottom part of the head for maximum control. As a player becomes more adept, the hand can slide further down, eventually ending up in the middle of the stick.

Step 1. Stand straight up in the dynamic ready position. With the head of your stick up by your ear, extend your arm forward so that the opening of the head of the stick is facing your partner and positioned at a 45-degree angle from your head. This placement of the stick allows you to see the ball and the head of your stick at the same time as it is protected from checks.

Step 2. Hold the stick with your hand just under the head keeping a loose and relaxed grip. Your bottom hand should be placed a few inches in front of the vertically hanging shaft, palm facing the stick, open and relaxed.

Step 3. Now have your partner throw a lacrosse ball into the head of the stick. Hold the stick loosely enough that the momentum of the ball entering the stick pushes the head of the stick, tilting it backwards. This will cause the shaft of the stick to tilt foreword as the head moves back. Catch the bottom of your stick with your bottom hand. If you do this properly, you will end up with the ball in the head and your stick back in the dynamic ready position.

Continue this drill until the player is comfortable catching with the top hand. Be sure to also practice this drill with the opposite hand. It can be frustrating at times, but developing skill with both hands early on is important to a player's later development. Push the limits of comfort while keeping the drill fun and functional. Be sure to watch for any bad habits, such as slapping at the ball with the head or pointing it too much toward the thrower.

Top-Hand Catching

FOR many young players the challenge of one-handed drills is simply an issue of strength. Many young players are handed heavy, long, adult-size sticks and told to play with them. Give the kids a break! As an aid in developing ability and confidence, it is sometimes good to start with a smaller stick, whether a cut down version or one of the many commercial ministicks produced. In addition, the use of a lighter sponge or tennis ball may help. Keep in mind that this is just a temporary adjunct to training with regulation equipment. Use these training tools perhaps as a warm-up device, and then progress to the normal equipment when confidence and skill has been achieved.

Bottom-Hand Catching

Another great drill to learn proper "soft hands" catching comes to us from the Canadian leagues. Indoor players use their bottom hands to control the stick, and so use a bottom-hand catching drill to enhance their abilities. Indeed the indoor players, with their ultra-narrow heads, have to be excellent at catching in order to play the game at all.

Step 1. Begin in the dynamic ready position, holding your stick vertically just in front of your head as with the first drill.

Step 2. Now let go of the top hand, and keep it loose and open a few inches behind your stick. Have your partner throw a ball into the head of the stick hard enough to tilt the head back.

Step 3. When the head of the stick moves backward from the force of the throw, "catch" the upper part of your stick with your open top hand. You should end up again in a dynamic ready position with the head of your stick by your ear.

This method forces you to use the bottom hand and to relinquish control of the stick from the top hand, a challenge, as we said, for many baseball-oriented American players. Keep the throws light and accurate, and this skill will develop rapidly and easily. Be sure to correct any mistakes, such as grabbing the stick with the top hand prior to the ball entering the head of the stick, or trying to flip the stick over so that the mesh points toward the ground. Part of what is being developed with this drill is confidence in the design of the stick. Many players look at the head and the mesh and do not initially understand that the opening of the basket can face forward without the ball dropping out. Once they practice this drill and see how "soft hand" catching creates a cushion, they will understand that the end position is slightly offset to the ground, thus keeping the ball secure in the bottom of the head. The unintuitive concept of catching with a lacrosse stick in the vertical position will become second nature.

Bottom-Hand Catching

Putting It All Together: Mastery in Catching

Now that you have drilled in the basic skills that make up catching, it is time to think about putting them together. Mastery involves the ability to fluidly and faultlessly combine many basics skills. Here is one master drill:

Step 1. To catch lacrosse ball begin in the dynamic ready position with the head of your stick by your ear.

Step 2. As the ball arrives push the head of your stick forward, using the top hand to align it with the trajectory of the ball. Remember to not "point" the head at the ball, but to place the open face of the head in the way of the on coming ball.

Step 3. Once the head is in position, relax the top hand and allow the ball to enter the mesh. As the ball hits the mesh, let the stick travel back to the starting position by your ear, cushioning the incoming pass in your mesh.

Step 4. At this point cradle to ensure full control of the ball and prepare to throw it back, but only after a full recovery and cushion to the ready position. This way we avoid slapping at and cradling the ball out of the air, a major mistake seen in many beginning players.

Always remember to catch first, cradle second. That way you will always maintain control over the ball.

The ultimate goal after mastering the basics is to be able to apply them in unconventional positions and while moving. This will take time to master, but the basics remain the same. The highest-level player can catch a pass with either hand equally well no matter how a where a pass is going. Catching a ball at your feet or at waist-level is a given when it comes to mastery in the game, but each time a pass is caught, remember that there must be an application of a "soft-hands" cushioning to pull it off. So strive to develop a soft catch by practicing both bottom- and top-hand catching as a warm up to any skill session or throwaround.

CHAPTER 21

THROWING

As you must in any ball sport that involves passing, it is imperative to cultivate the ability to move the ball from player to player with speed, accuracy, and efficiency. Learning how to throw a lacrosse ball is learning how to operate a machine, called a stick, in order to move the ball from point A to point B through the air. The act of throwing converts your stick into a lever that propels your ball toward another player. The action and physics are exactly the same as a catapult. The tricky part is to get the stick/body interface working at an optimal level so that throwing becomes easy.

American and Canadian players have evolved somewhat different styles of throwing because they come from different backgrounds in hockey and baseball. The hockey-based method, also called "bottom throwing," utilizes the bottom hand as a major control over the stick, using a pulling action to move the stick forward and to propel the ball. This bottom-hand method allows for quick passing and is analogous to shooting, which will be covered later. The top hand in the Canadian throw acts as a guide for accuracy, adding little to the actual propulsion of the ball. The American method of throwing, also known as "top throwing," harkens back to a baseball throw, in which the majority of the propulsion comes from the top hand pushing the stick forward. Combine these two and add variations, and you have the ultimate throwing method, but first we must practice and master the basics.

Throwing power comes from the body and is transferred via the arms to the lever that is the stick. Always keep your head up, arms extended and relaxed while you throw. This will allow your body to move naturally through the throwing motion and to develop proper form and perfect muscle memory. Practice the individual parts drills and complete the throw with both hands. Eventually you will learn to throw from any position your stick may be in, whether it is underhand, sidearm, or behind the back. These previously "advanced" stick skills are now the norm for every player.

The growing repertoire of throws a present day lacrosse player must master is incredible to say the least. Prior to the lacrosse revolution created by the Gait brothers, lacrosse players maintained some basic throwing skills such as the overhand pass, sidearm, and, if feeling really fancy, an underhand flip. Nowadays one must master at a minimum the following throws: overhead, three-quarter, sidearm, underhand, behind-the-head, flip, shovel, and the backhand (also known as Canadian). But every throw begins with the basic overhand method of throwing we have previously described. Once you have gotten confident in your ability with the basic throw, try the three-quarter-position throw, which is simply an overhead throw that comes at a slight angle and then begin to practice all the others, throwing from every possible angle.

Top-Hand Throwing

Step 1. Assume the dynamic ready position, gripping the stick in a prethrow tennis grip about midway up the shaft.

Step 2. Step forward with your front foot as if pitching a baseball, and torque your body so that your stick side shoulder turns toward your throwing target.

Step 3. As you start your throw, allow the head of the stick to follow through as you break your wrist letting the bottom half of the shaft to move backward. When you are done the head of your stick should be pointing toward your target and the butt-end of the stick should be in line with your throwing arm.

Practice this method of throwing until you can hit your target consistently. Make sure to practice using both left and right hands.

Bottom-Hand Throwing

Step 1. Begin in the dynamic ready position holding your stick in pre-throw mode with both hands.

Step 2. Step forward and pull your stick with your bottom hand.

Step 3. As you begin your throw, let your top hand give a little take-off push in order to aim your throw, but after this let the bottom hand take over pulling the stick and propelling the ball forward. When you are done the head of the stick should be pointing at your intended target.

Putting it All Together

Now that you have skills for throwing with both your top and bottom hands, combine the two movements into a simultaneous push/pull. This in conjunction with proper body torque will allow you to perform perfect, accurate throws. Now begin to practice the basic overhand throw at first. After mastering this you can move on to the three-quarter, sidearm, underhand, behind the head, and backhand throws. Each use the same basic mechanism for launching the ball out of your stick.

Overhand Throw

Step 1. Begin in the dynamic ready position holding your stick in prethrow mode with both hands.

Step 2. Hold your stick high with the shaft up by your ear. Point the butt-end of your stick at your target, sighting down the shaft as if it were a rifle.

Step 3. Step forward and allow your body to turn utilizing the combined push/pull throwing movement. Allow the head of your stick to travel straight over your shoulder.

Step 4. Follow through with your throw ending with the head of your stick pointing to your target.

Three-Quarter Throw

Step 1. Begin in the dynamic ready position holding your stick in prethrow mode with both hands.

Step 2. Hold your stick high with the shaft by your throwing-side shoulder.

Step 3. Step forward and allow your body to turn utilizing the combined push/pull throwing movement. Allow the head of your stick to travel on a three-quarter arc just off of your throwing-side shoulder.

Step 4. Follow through with your throw ending with the head of your stick pointing to your target.

Sidearm Throw

Step 1. Begin in the dynamic ready position holding your stick in prethrow mode with both hands.

Step 2. Hold your stick at midlevel by your throwing-side hip.

Step 3. Step forward and allow your body to turn utilizing the combined push/pull throwing movement. Allow the head of your stick to travel horizontally.

Step 4. Follow through with your throw ending with the head of your stick pointing to your target.

Underhand Throw

Step 1. Begin in the dynamic ready position holding your stick in prethrow mode with both hands.

Step 2. Hold your stick below midlevel below your throwing-side hip.

Step 3. Step forward and allow your body to turn utilizing the combined push/pull throwing movement. Allow the head of your stick to travel upward.

Step 4. Follow through with your throw ending with the head of your stick pointing to your target.

Behind-the-Head Throw

This is one of the trickier throws in lacrosse. It is also called a behind the back throw. During your author's high school playing days this throw was a no-no and grounds for getting you pulled out of a game by your coach. Now it is a staple of lacrosse players worldwide. To perform the behind the head throw.

Step 1. Begin in the dynamic ready position holding your stick in a prethrow grip.

Step 2. Lean forward across your body, clearing your head, and bend slightly at the waist.

Step 3. With the shaft vertical and parallel to your body, pull with your top hand toward your stick-side shoulder while pushing with your bottom hand. When you are done your stick should be vertical and the ball should release right behind your head. Remember to bend forward so that the stick can travel behind your head to your stick-side shoulder. Do not try and "bend" the stick around your shoulders for this will change the release point of the ball.

Backhand/Canadian Throw

Step 1. Begin in the dynamic ready position holding your stick in prethrow mode with both hands.

Step 2. Turn your body and bring the stick in a vertical position to the opposite side of your body without switching hands. Make sure to turn the head of the stick so that the opening is facing your target.

Step 3. Step forward and allow your body to turn utilizing the combined push/pull throwing movement. Allow the head of your stick to travel forward.

Step 4. Follow through with your throw ending with the head of your stick pointing to your target.

CHAPTER 22

PASSING

You'll notice that we've been using the word "throwing," not "passing," so far in this section. Passing is throwing, but something else as well. A pass is a throw to another team member who is trying to catch it in a game situation. That is, while he's moving and under pressure from defenders. The skill of passing is paramount to success on the playing field because a pass moves the ball around much faster than anyone can run. A good pass immediately changes of the flow of the game and opens up opportunities to score.

Passing takes a greater amount of skill than throwing. As a passer, you must be able to gauge the distances of a moving target (your teammate) while adjusting for your own momentum on the run. The first step in developing passing skills is to master the basic throwing techniques. These throwing techniques were the subject of the preceding chapter. Once you've mastered them standing still, you'll need to start practicing them while on the move. The easiest way to practice is simply to never stay put while throwing and catching. Start with short lateral passes to your partner who runs parallel to you. Shuffle your feet as you throw back and forth.

When this becomes easy to do, begin circling one another while throwing and catching. Make sure to maintain a good dynamic ready position and keep your eyes and stick up and watch the ball all the way into your stick. Perform a controlled cradle and give a good solid pass back to your partner, making sure to follow through all the way to your target.

MATT BROWN'S TIPS ON PASSING

There are several ways to pass the ball from one teammate to another. Professional lacrosse players make it look very easy, but passing might just be the hardest skill of the game. The reason why I feel that passing is one of the hardest skills in lacrosse is because players develop extremely bad habits at an early age. There is just not enough proper knowledge of the sport out there right now, so learning the basics can be a challenge.

The overhand pass is the first pass that every lacrosse player should learn. There are two ways I practice making the overhand pass. The first way is to stand around 15 feet away from a brick or cement wall and focus on hitting one spot on the wall, pushing with your top hand while simultaneously pulling with your bottom hand. This kind of accuracy passing should be practiced every day in order to increase your skill and comfort level. The more accurate your passing is, the more effective a player you will be. Your goal is to place the ball into the head of your teammate's stick, making it easy for him or her to catch. Your accuracy in passing is key to achieving this; so hit the wall focusing on consistency in pass placement.

The second way is to get really close to the wall, about 3 feet away, and play pass with the wall again. This proximity to the wall forces you to not follow through with your passes and also work on your cushioning when you catch. In basic skills throwing, you typically follow through. But in game situations you will find that there are times when being able to short-stroke a pass is better suited. A perfect example is when you have a defender right on top of you, and following through on your pass would result in him hitting your stick, causing the ball to go somewhere you didn't want it to.

In general, it is best while in the open field to follow through on your passes. This way you get more accuracy and farther distance out of each throw.

As you begin to get better at throwing and catching while moving, you can begin to accelerate the pace of both your movement and your passes. You can also add more people to the mix. Instead of just one passing partner, add a third. This way you have two people to whom you can throw or receive a pass. Many Division 1 teams practice this way, using moving triangles of three players: defense on the outside using long passes (20-40 yards), middies in the intermediate 8-10 yard passes, and attack closest to the center or around the goal using quick short passes. This way your team can all practice at the same time and get maximum touches on the ball at the proper ranges for each position played.

Many types of passes are called for during a game. One of the most challenging is the over the shoulder pass. This pass is used to throw to a player moving away from the passer. Typically it is thrown by a goalie to a midfielder or defenseman after a save has been made. This pass is much like a quarterback's pass to a wide receiver breaking down field. It must be thrown not at the player, but ahead of them, to spot where they will be in two or three strides as they continue to run. When the ability of a passer to "lead" a running player is matched with the ability of a player to catch the ball over-the-shoulder without breaking stride, the opportunity for a fast break is created. Fast breaks are one of the important and exciting parts of the game.

Becoming a good passer will earn you a spot on any team. Becoming a great passer will help take you and your team to the top. The best way to become great passer is to pass, pass, and pass. Practice everyday. Practice varying the angles to your partner or teammates. Learn to "lead" targets moving away or laterally to you. Try to place your pass on the head of your teammate's stick when he is cutting toward you. If you master these skills, you will be one step further to becoming a complete lacrosse player.

Putting All the Skills Together: Playing Wall Ball

Now that you have a basic throw, catch, and cradle down, it is time to put them together. A great way to train is to just go out with a friend and throw around. This can be a bit frustrating if both people are beginners. A great way to train solo is wall ball. Every great lacrosse player has spent countless hours throwing a lacrosse ball against a wall. With wall ball you can practice all of the throwing and catching without a partner. It is a time for personal perfection in technique. There are myriad drills that can be done against the wall—a basic throw and catch, split drills, even quick stick drills—all of which should be practiced daily for the entirety of your lacrosse career. Here are some examples of drills you can do on the wall.

DRILLS:

1. 1 hand: catch and 1cradle
2. 2 hands: catch and 1 cradle
3. 2 hands: quick stick
4. 2 hands: split drill (catch right, switch and throw left, then catch left, switch, and throw right)
5. 2 hands: catch, face dodge, and throw
6. 2 hands: catch, fake, and throw

For more advanced players try the following:
1. 2 hands: cross body
2. 2 hands: behind the back
3. 2 hands: running along the wall throwing and catching.

One caveat about wall ball is to make sure that the wall you are throwing on is made of brick or cinder block so that you will not cause any damage. Also, make sure you have permission to use the wall in this manner. You are an ambassador of the sport and it is simply "not cool" to chuck lacrosse balls against walls that you do not own, such as school buildings and the like. In this day of stucco and aluminum garage doors it may actually be difficult to find an appropriate wall for wall ball. The solution is a rebounding trainer made by many of the major lacrosse manufacturers. This setup provides a target that rebounds the ball back to the thrower. It is well worth the cost of the item and it can be found being used in most college lacrosse programs and in the backyards of many players, both young and old.

CHAPTER 23

DODGING

Dodging is how a player moves past defenders while carrying the ball toward the goal, and how a player gets "open" in off-ball play. There are many different kinds of dodging, and each involves some different skills. When to use a dodge, or even which dodge works best for individual players and match-ups, is something only experience and trial and error can determine. In order to give you the most options on the field, each dodge will be examined and explained so that you may develop your dodging skills to their utmost. Remember, no matter which position you play—attack, midfield, defense, and even goalie—at some point you will be face to face with a defender trying to strip the ball from you, or to at least impede your progress up field. Dodging is the key to getting safely past these impediments while maintaining possession and control of the ball. There are three key factors in dodging: body position, stick protection, and acceleration.

BODY POSITION

The first thing to pay attention to in dodging is your body position relative to the defender and to the goal itself. When dodging, your ultimate aim is to get as close to the front of the goal as possible, or at least to get to a position relative to the goal that will give you an angle for a shot or a feed to an open player. Your line of approach toward the goal will depend on your starting position on the

field. If you are dodging an attackman directly behind the goal or a midfielder out in front of the goal, your orientation to the goal will be different. Nevertheless, your aim is to get past the defenseman and into a position to shoot or pass the ball. This is important for off-ball players as well because dodging will allow them to get open and receive a pass from another player. The off-ball dodge is all about creating separation from your defender. Separation allows you to receive a pass safely while positioning yourself to make an offensive drive or shot toward the goal. Judging your position relative to the goal becomes somewhat obvious as one plays the game. It is the position relative to a defender that is more challenging, and that realistically is dependent upon the individual skills of both the offensive and defensive players.

Your body position relative to your defender is important for completing a successful dodge. In fact, your body position relative to the defender is the key to successful dodging, because it helps to freeze your defender in place and allows you to take advantage of the reaction time gap. Reaction time, measured in milliseconds, is the neurologically determined interval in which a person can see and recognize movement and then begin to actually react to it. It takes approximately 250 milliseconds or one-quarter of a second for this process to be completed. So if you move quickly enough, without telegraphing your intentions to your defender, you will start with a one-quarter second edge in movement. An average person can move 7 feet a second. This means that if you freeze your opponent and take proper advantage of the reaction gap you can get nearly a 2-foot lead, more than enough to get a shot off or force a slide from a secondary defender.

So how does one freeze an opponent? That is where the body positioning comes in. Ideally you want your defender to face you squarely so that they must choose which side to go first. Fortunately, being upright bipedal creatures, we must slightly offset in order to maintain balance in all four directions. This offset will be your clue. If your defender has his left foot slightly forward, he can be more easily taken advantage of by going in that direction. Since he will be less able to follow quickly, your dodge would be to the defender's left side. This, of course, is dependent upon his ability and your ability to freeze him in place before you dodge. This is best done by driving directly to the centerline of your defender, being careful to time your dodge for the last possible second before, or even during, his initial check against you. One can center up on a defender by driving hard at him and performing a quick hop-switch before accelerating past. These skills should be familiar from your agility training and are the basis for the previously described split drill.

STICK POSITION

Once you have moved into the dodge, you must focus on stick position. Indeed, stick positioning, which translates into stick protection, must occur simultaneously with your initial move. It may, in the case of the face dodge, be the setup for the dodge itself. Regardless of which dodge is performed, it is imperative that your stick be protected while you are performing these quick change of direction moves. Keeping your stick in line with the center of your body offers the most protection from checks by placing the most amount of body mass between defenders and your stick. However, it will not work if you stay squared up with your defender. The basic rule of stick protection when keeping the stick at the center line is to always have your shoulder facing your defender. For example, if a player is dodging to the right and his stick is in his right hand, then the player must turn his body to the right and place his left shoulder between the defender and the stick. This offers the most protection when dodging. Practicing this is vital. Otherwise a player will find himself losing the ball as he tries to move past the defender, or even losing his stick if a good check is placed on him.

ACCELERATION

The last and most important element for developing ultimate dodging skill is acceleration. The concepts of the reaction time gap, freezing your opponent, and protecting your stick are useless if you cannot accelerate away from the defender you have just dodged. It is the mistake of many youth players to pull off a dodge without accelerating past their defender. Indeed, often you can see players "beat" their man only to run back into coverage. Some players even lack good dodging skills but make up for that with blinding speed and quick acceleration that takes full advantage of the reaction gap. Needles to say, when practicing your dodging, make sure that you accelerate quickly past your defender. Using the hop-switch move will greatly enhance your ability to pull this off.

BASIC DODGES

There are myriad new dodges and stick protection moves being performed on lacrosse fields and turf rinks all around the globe. The innovations in dodging and movement are coming at an amazing pace. This is due in part to the modern stick designs, which seem to defy physics in their ability to hold a ball, and in part to the increased creativity and athletic ability of new players. In one unforgettable display, Mikey Powell pulled off a full front-flip dodge before driving to the goal during a game. Showy, yes, but it is an example of the almost limitless possibilities for dodges. Nonetheless, the basic dodges described here are the bread and butter of dodging ability, and their mastery will give you a strong base from which to work.

As with every skill section of this book, these drills will help you develop the skills we discussed. In addition to practicing your dodging individually, you should try dodging during longer drills, such as the slalom and ladder drills outlined in the agility section. For middies, the split drill (page 66) will be a great asset, and for attackers the reverse slalom (page 216) will do just fine. D-poles should have their face dodges down in order to protect those long sticks. In addition to these drills, you should use a mirror to practice dodging, watching to see whether you are properly protecting your stick. Another great drill is to perform one-on-ones where you play offense and defense against a teammate and practice dodging in a real setting. Make sure to do this wearing proper footwear and full pads in order to eliminate injuries.

Outlined on the following pages are a few basic dodges that all players should learn. Each is used for a specific time and place on the field.

© Dugald Munro

Face Dodge

One of the simplest dodges is the face dodge. This dodge is typically used when a defender is coming aggressively toward you with his stick high in order to check you. As the defender moves toward you, turn your body, passing the stick in front of your face to your opposite ear, placing your shoulder and helmet between you and the defender. As you do this, accelerate past the check and uncoil your body back to your starting position. This dodge is most often seen when an offensive player is winding up to shoot and a defender comes out aggressively to meet them. It can also be used very effectively while driving on a defender. The Canadian box players, who are reticent to switch hands while playing, use this to great effect. For players who are not yet comfortable switching hands with their stick, this will be the most effective dodge you can learn.

Split Dodge

The split dodge is the most common dodge seen from the midfield position. There are two versions: a true split dodge and a false split. The true split dodge is performed while driving hard to the goal against a defender who is squared up with you. Drive directly toward the defender and switch hands with your stick as you accelerate past. For example, if you are holding the stick in your right hand, dodge to the left of your defender while switching your stick to the left side as you move. Be sure to turn the opposite shoulder so that you keep the stick protected. Once past the defender, you may switch the stick back or keep it in your opposite hand. Be sure to "freeze" your opponent by driving straight at him, and only switch your stick and dodge at the last possible moment before getting checked.

The False Split

The false split is basically a fake. Run toward your defender and give a little shoulder fake, as if you are going to switch hands. But this time keep it in the original hand and acceler-ate past. Be sure to keep your head up, so you can see the field for a potential shot on goal or pass to a teammate.

Roll Dodge

The roll dodge is typically used when either the split or face dodge has failed, and your man has kept up with you. In this case drive him in one direction, and then perform a hop-switch (as practiced in the slalom drills) and roll past him, while protecting your stick. Make sure that you accelerate past the defender once you have switched direction, driving toward the goal. Otherwise, you will just be running back and forth and making no progress toward the goal. One trick for protecting your stick during a roll dodge is to keep it close to your chest while rolling. This offers great protection and can even keep the ball in your stick as you roll through multiple defenders.

Belt Buckle Switch

In addition to that, one can perform a belt-buckle switch while rolling. As you turn, drop the head of the stick down to your belt line as you roll. This protects it from stick checks and gets it out of the way during the dodge. Another alternative is not to switch hands while rolling, but to keep the stick low and in between your legs, as if riding a broom. The roll dodge is a staple for close attackmen driving against long stick defenders. It is a great tool for quick and agile players who can use their speed and change of direction to "shake off" a defender and accelerate past him.

Bull Dodge

The bull dodge is an "old school" move that physically challenges your defender to stay on his feet. Simply put, the bull dodge is a controlled collision with your defender in an attempt to knock him down or off balance so you can speed by. Typically done against a smaller player by large opponents, it can be used effectively against anyone with less-than-perfect footwork. Drive aggressively toward your opponent and pick a side to dodge to. Make sure to make contact with your body against his dodging-side shoulder.

Do not go head-to-head, but "bump" him so that he must use energy to remain balanced. This little disruption will allow you to then take advantage of the reaction time gap and accelerate past or through the opposing player and toward the goal.

ONE of the drills that is used by many offensive professionals in the NLL is the three step drill. This drill is more of a rule of movement than a true drill. It states that you take no more then three steps in any direction before changing your route. So if you are off-ball and waiting to get a pass, work your defender by using this drill. If you have the ball and are looking to feed or want to set your defender up for a dodge to the goal, use this to keep him off balance and guessing what you will do next. To see the effectiveness of this concept in practice, watch any NLL game in which the Arizona Sting's "Dangerous" Dan Dawson is playing. He is a master of this method of quick and efficient movement that keeps his defenders wondering what such a big man will do next.

DODGING TIPS FROM MATT BROWN

Dodging is the name of the game in lacrosse for one-on-one play. An offensive player dodges his defender on an attempt to make an offensive opportunity for himself or his teammates. There are many different ways to dodge your defender. For example, many players have traditionally used a quick speed move down the side of the field or alley. Today, players have come up with new ways of beating their defenders. One of the more innovative methods is called smash mouth, a very successful way of dodging. Smash mouth dodging consists of you, the offensive player, initiating contact with your defender, then switching direction depending on the defenders reaction. This is a very aggressive method of dodging that I feel is the key to being a good dodger. It forces the defender to be on the defensive since you are initiating the move on offense. The best dodgers in the world combine physical moves with changes of speed and changes of direction, with either rollbacks and/or hitches, in a quick, aggressive, and dynamic mode of play. It's how I have earned a living in the professional game of lacrosse.

NOTE: For demonstration purposes only, this dodge is performed by a female. However, currently this dodge is only legal in men's lacrosse.

Bull Dodge

CHAPTER 24

SHOOTING

Shooting is the thing offensive players live for. Simply put, you can't win games unless you score, and you can't score unless you shoot. It is a mantra of many coaches that offensive players should be "shooters first, passers second." Now that does not mean that every time you handle the ball you must go for the goal. On the contrary, it means that you must play a smart, pass-oriented game, but when an opportunity presents itself, take the shot!

Shooting requires the highest level of throwing skill. The intention, velocity, and placement of a shoot distinguish it from a pass. The intention, of course, is to get the ball past the goalie and into the net. This is not as easy as it may sound because defenders and the goalkeeper will try to prevent this. The way a shooter attempts to overcome the defense is a mix of shot velocity and shot placement.

In general, you want to shoot the ball as fast as you can and place it in areas of the goal most difficult for a goalie to stop, specifically the upper and lower corners of the goal. Prior to shooting you may also want to offer a fake of some sort to make the goalie react prematurely to your shot. You may try to dodge to a position on the field where you are close enough to the goal to "beat" the goalie.

No matter how you try to increase your chances of scoring, the basic ability to shoot at long, middle, and close range is needed.

The kind of shot you are offered will depend on where you usually are on the field and, to that extent, on the position you play. For example, if you play close or crease attack, you may rarely shoot from farther than a few yards from the goal, while as a midfielder you may end up shooting a large percentage of your shots from 10-plus yards. No matter your position or shooting preference, it all starts with an understanding of the basic mechanics of the shot itself.

There are many ways to shoot a lacrosse ball. Starting from basic throwing techniques, it is an advanced skill that should be developed to the level at which you can shoot a ball from every possible stick position to every area of the goal. However, just as everyone must learn to walk before they can run, so here we will learn and practice the basics of shooting using the overhand method. After this is mastered, the three-quarter, sidearm, underhand, quick stick, and behind the head shoots can be developed, but it all starts with the basic overhand shooting.

Basic Overhand Shooting

In order to better understand the basic overhand shot we will again break it down into its component parts. First is the position of your hands on the stick. Depending on your preference your hands will be much closer together than when you throw a pass. This lower position on the stick allows the stick to be pulled with greater force as you turn your hips while shooting. Your lower hand should be providing the majority of the grip on the stick while your top hand will provide more of directional control. Do not over grip with the top hand, or this will cause you to "push" with the top hand instead of pulling with the bottom hand, which is what you want for full power shots. Keep you arms relaxed and extended so that the stick is positioned high and behind your body. The positioning of your stick in relation to your body is important because it places it in a position where it is protected from checks and hides the head of your stick from the goalie. Check your beginning position form in a mirror if need be and make corrections. Be sure to keep the stick head up so that you do not drop the ball. Many youth players believe that you have to "cock" you stick back in order to get power. That is not true. The power will come from your hips and waist, not your arms. Pulling your arms too far back will allow the stick's head to tilt down and the ball to fall out. Trust the high positioning of the stick and pull hard with your bottom hand as you torque your hips.

BODY POSITIONING

In order to crank out "white hot rips" while shooting, you must develop comfort in using your body to generate power. Because you will be using your legs, hips, and waist to torque your body and drive your arms and stick forward, you must position your body precisely. Position it so that the natural twisting movement will be able to generate maximum force while driving the ball where you want it to go. A good way to see this is to observe a major league baseball pitcher. When throwing to the plate, the pitcher stands sideways to the batter and not facing him. This positioning of the shoulder and hip 90-degrees from the target allows the body to twist into the pitch. The ball is whipped forward and released. This is exactly the same mechanics needed for shooting. If you watch a baseball pitcher in slow motion, you will see that the body generates the power. The arm holding the ball is just along for the ride, directing the ball but not propelling it. The arm itself is a source of direction, not power, for the pitch. This is all closely analogous to the way you should handle your stick. As we said before, you must position your off-stick shoulder in the direction you want to shoot. Squaring up to the goal and shooting that way will send your ball wide of the net time and again.

Now you may be wondering how you throw a ball at something while facing away from it. The answer, once again, can be found in the baseball pitcher's motion. The pitcher's front foot steps forward. When your front foot steps forward and toward the goal, this forces your body to turn toward it. This torquing motion is what generates the full body power that can launch a lacrosse shot at over 100 miles per hour—as fast as the fastest major leaguers pitch. One drill that you can do to get used to this motion is the face-away ball throw.

RELEASE POINT

When shooting a lacrosse ball it is important to have an understanding of the release point of your stick. The release point is the point at which the ball travels off of the mesh, specifically, the throwing strings. This is usually determined by how the stick itself is strung and, more precisely, the location of the deepest part of the pocket in relation to the shooting strings. Every stick is slightly different. If a stick has too much "whip," it will often force the ball down toward the ground. If the pocket has little or no "whip," the ball will usually release early and too high. Work with your stick to find the "sweet spot" where the ball settles naturally. Know where your release point is when passing and when shooting. If it does not feel right, then adjust the shooting strings until you get the release you want. Otherwise you may develop the most powerful shot in the world, but one that goes everywhere except the goal.

Face-Away Ball Throw

Step 1. Stand with your back toward your partner and your stick with a ball in the mesh in front of you. Make sure to keep the stick at 45 degrees to the ground so the ball will not fall out.

Step 2. While keeping your stick in that position, step with your off-stick leg toward your partner behind you. For example, if you are holding the stick in the right hand, step your left foot back and towards your partner, goal, or wall. As you take this step, be sure to keep your stick where it is.

Step 3. As you step toward your target, allow your body to turn toward it and pull your stick up and over your shoulder. Release the ball toward your target and follow through to the ground with the head of your stick.

Though this is an exaggeration of the shooting movement, it will help you to feel the way the body controls the shot and to get used to stepping and turning without pushing your stick.

FOLLOW THROUGH AND FOCUS

Once you have the basic feel for the body shot and the release point of your stick, it is important to allow your shot to follow through to your target. Follow through is both a physical and mental act. The physical part is the continuation of your stick through the release point of the shot. That part is pretty simple. The mental aspect is in the planning of the shot and the shot placement. This is focusing on where you want the shot to go in the net in relation to the goalie trying to stop it.

At the beginning levels you need to focus most on the physical part of the shot and getting the ball into the center of the goal. After you have this down, your focus will shift to shooting at a specific area of the goal, the upper or lower corners or hip level pipes. Eventually you'll start planning to shoot around a determined goalie. One of the tricks you'll learn is being able to see "past" or behind the goalie and into the open parts of the net. As humans we are habituated to focus on things and people in the foreground, not what's behind them. A great exercise is to have a partner stand in the goal and stare at them, then change your focus to around and beyond them to the net. Switch back and forth, focusing on them, then on the net. This will help get you to the point at which you are always aware of the open spots of the net, while simultaneously tracking the goalie's position in the net.

Hand, stick, and body positioning coupled with a good front step, body toque, and proper follow through are the keys to developing a great shot. But with all things physical it must be practiced many times, requiring a dedicated player to have access to a goal or some form of net at which to shoot. Nets and goals can be purchased from virtually every one of the major equipment manufactures at competitive process.

FRESH BALLS VS. POTATOES

To many beginning players, a lacrosse ball is just that, a ball—something to catch, cradle, shoot, and throw. This blissful ignorance is not something that a serious player can continue to cultivate. A player must understand how a ball is made and how it will perform over the stages of its useful life. The basic design of a lacrosse ball is universal: round, rubbery, and "sticky" on the outside when new. This "stickiness" begins to wear down as a ball is thrown and caught, eventually polishing it to a smooth, shiny exterior. This worn-out smoothness does not allow the ball to sit properly in the stick, nor does it allow the ball to stick to the mesh. It also changes the release point of the ball. Like a worn out tennis ball, a lacrosse ball loses its performance capabilities with wear. Though good for the budget, practicing with old and shiny balls, called potatoes or cancer balls by pros like the Arizona Sting's Dan Dawson, can actually be a detriment in training. Keep a stock of new balls on hand for shooting and passing practice. "Potatoes" can be used to make pocket pounders or to play with your dog. It may seem nothing but a detail, but it really can negatively effect your shooting practice.

SHOOTING DRILLS

A shooting workout, if done properly, should leave you tired and winded. When you are first learning to shoot, place yourself close to the goal or net, and do not concern yourself too much with shot placement. Focus on good form and developing a hard, fast shot. Once you have that down, you can back away from the net and begin placing your shots. Good training tools are the many goal targets that are sold by equipment manufactures. These are items that block large parts of the net and only allow the ball to enter the goal in the "high probability" areas such as upper and lower corners, off hip level side and the five hold between a goalie's legs. It is a great way to practice your shot placement once your basic shooting is down pat. A sample-shooting workout follows.

Overhand Shooting

Step 1. Begin in the dynamic ready position.

Step 2. Place your hands on your stick as if ready to pass, but this time drop the top hand down lower than usual.

Step 3. Point your off-stick shoulder toward the part of the goal where you want the ball to go. Extend your arms up and out from your body, feeling the ball in your stick as you take a big step forward (a little longer than a basic throw first step).

Step 4. Explosively rotate your waist and allow your arms to begin moving your stick forward, making sure to stay relaxed. Allow your arms and stick to whip forward as you continue your upper body rotation.

Step 5. Let your stick continue through all the way to the ground. When you are done, your stick-side shoulder should be pointing to the goal. Your stick should have followed through past the point at which you released the ball. This will result in a strong fast shot to the middle of the goal.

Shooting Drill

Step 1. Place 10 balls in 10 piles at varying distances and angles to the goal from 2–15 yards.

Step 2. Begin at the closest pile and shoot your favorite shot from this spot into the goal.

Step 3. Rest for a minute or so and move to the next pile.

The goal is hard, fast, high-quality shots that hit their intended targets. Make sure to practice placement shots at close range, hard lining shots at medium range, and hard bounce shots at long range.

Once you have mastered this, begin shooting from these same distances while on the run, while being fed, or after picking up a ground ball. At the advanced level you can do all of these drills using the full arsenal of shots in the contemporary player's book of tricks. Use overhand, underhand, behind the neck, quick stick, and between the legs shots. Invent and use a shot solely your own. The basic goal is 100 shots in a training session, aiming for a 100 percent shot-to-target completion. Remember to keep good form. Have fun and shoot hard and accurately.

MATT BROWN'S TIPS ON SHOOTING

Being an attackman, shooting is a large part of my responsibilities on the field. Shooting differs from passing because when passing, you are assisting someone, your teammate, to catch the ball. Shooting is exactly the opposite; you are trying to prevent someone on the other team, the goalie, from catching the ball.

One of the biggest mistakes many youth and high school players make is that they try to shoot the ball as hard as they can each and every shot. Some times this works, but most of the time it results in missing the net. The key to shooting is not how hard you can throw the ball, but how deceptive and quick you are in releasing it. A field lacrosse goal is 6 by 6 feet. That is a lot of room in which to put a 3-inch diameter ball. The biggest factor is that there is a goalie defending that 6 by 6-foot goal, and getting the ball around him is a challenge. Being deceptive will achieve a higher percentage of goals than shooting just with pure raw power and speed. Making a goalie think you are going to shoot the ball to one place and then putting it in another is the better way to go. This may sound pretty obvious and simple, but many players have problems doing it. Pump fakes, eye fakes, and body English are all ways to help deceive a cagey goalie. Practice and a find a method that works best for you, remembering that deception and shot placement are more important for scoring that anything else you can do.

As a professional lacrosse player, I train hard every day. Simply put, the only way you get better at shooting is to shoot, shoot, and shoot. When I was younger I would spend many hours every day in my back yard just shooting. There were even times when neighbors would complain, telling me to stop because they couldn't handle the sound of the ball hitting the goal posts at midnight. That is the kind of commitment to practice it takes to become a pro. When I coach kids, I recommend that they practice shooting in all different ways, because the more ways you can shoot, the more deceptive you will be. The ability to shoot from any angle and with either hand gives you additional ways to put the ball past the goalie and into the back of the net.

PART IV

· ·

DEFENSE

New Jersey Pride's Rob Scherr defends the goal.

CHAPTER 25

DEFENSIVE SKILLS

"Every player plays defense" is the mantra of coaches worldwide. Even attackmen, the offensive wizards of the field, turn into defenders when they try to prevent the defensive unit from clearing the ball out of the zone. So, whatever your position, it is essential for you to develop the basic defensive skills that allow you to turn defender at a moment's notice.

Offensive players should become students of the defense in order to better understand the defenses they must overcome. Many offensive players believe that playing defense is easy. It's not. In fact, it takes better conditioning, quicker reactions, and increased physicality to play quality one-on-one defense. Team defense takes an even greater level of cooperation and coordination to bring off.

In this chapter we will focus on the basics of individual defensive play. These include body positioning relative to the offensive player, physical play (holds, pushes, and hits), and checking.

BODY POSITIONING

The single most important defensive skill is body positioning. Simply put, it is the job of every defender to place their body between the offensive player with the ball and the goal. This requires a constant awareness of your position relative to the goal wherever you are on the field of play. In addition, it demands that you instinctively set yourself at an angle to a player with the ball that will deny

him a straight run or shot at the goal. This is called "cutting the field." For example, if you are playing defense against a wing attackman, you would face away from the goal with your body angled up field to cut off his direct route to the open front of the goal. This position does leave an opportunity for the attackman to beat you to the back end of the goal, but that is tactically acceptable, since shooting from behind the goal is not as great a threat as a shot from in front.

This sort of positioning is best practiced on the field and will depend in part on the type of team defense and slide packages that your team is using. Therefore we will not say a lot more about it here. More important is the man-on-man positioning you adopt relative to the player you are defending against. Here we should recall the concept of a reaction time gap. Remember that a person can move approximately 2 feet in the quarter second before you will even register the movement. Keeping a body position that will buy you this time and distance is critical. That is where using your stick or pushing come into play. Whether you have a short stick or the long stick of a defender, your use of the stick to keep an offensive player at a distance will get you back this critical distance. You force the offensive player to move far enough away from you that you will be able to react to them.

We will now learn three ways to keep your ideal defensive distance: drop step, impact push, and hip poke.

Drop Step

The drop step is a footwork method that allows a defensive player to keep distance on an offensive player trying to dodge by. The drop step can be used in open field play or while a player is driving against you. Either way, you need to establish your positioning on him. The drop step is actually just like it sounds, a quick rearward step that allows you to essentially reset your defensive dynamic ready position further back from a moving offender. It can be used in conjunction with a hop-switch in order to increase the speed with which you reestablish your position. One of the best drills for developing this ability has already been covered. Do you remember the slalom drill? We are going to reuse the slalom drill, but for defense we will do it backwards. As you run backwards to the cone, hop-switch and run or shuffle back to the next cone, and switch again.

This is a great way to develop the drop step for defenders. Once this basic move is mastered, add in the stick positioning and eventually an offensive player coming toward you. The drop step is only the beginning, since it is evident that a defender cannot play great defense by continuing to give up ground to an offensive player driving to the goal. On the contrary, the drop step only resets the defenders body position so that he may now use other tools to keep an offensive player at bay, specifically, the impact push.

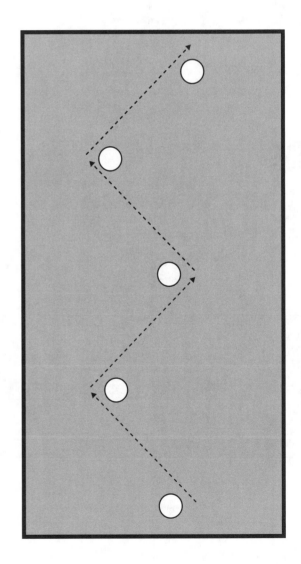

Impact Push

The impact push is a version of the old-fashioned push check, but done a little more forcefully, as the name implies. The impact push is intended to push an offensive player away. It must be performed legally, using the padded area of the gloves and not the stick itself. To do so with your stick is to perform an illegal check called a crosscheck. Crosschecking is both dangerous and unsportsmanlike. The impact push, done properly, will move the attacker away from the defender, while allowing the defender to maintain his balance. The impact push is performed with a lightening-quick motion that is directed from the center line of the body to the shoulder of the offensive player. The impact orientation allows a defender both to make contact with force and to break contact with equal quickness. This keeps a defensive player from "leaning" on the attacker, causing either a push-from-behind penalty or sacrificing his balance and allowing an offensive player to dodge around it.

To perform it properly, line up on another player and have him drive toward you. While running with him, allow your hands to come together on your stick at the center of your chest. Quickly and forcefully drive both hands forward, making contact with the padded portions of your gloves only. Once contact is made, immediately pull your hands back. Repeat the move if necessary.

Impact Push

A great drill is to practice this against a barrier like a chain-link fence. Shuffle laterally to the fence and apply quick impact pushes, then recover. Now do the same thing while running laterally to the fence. The impact of the push should shake the fence but allow you to keep your balance.

Another drill can be done using a football tackling shield. Have a coach run alongside you holding the shield. When he gets too close, apply an impact push to the shield. It should push him away. Be careful not to lean into the push or you will lose balance.

Checks

Once an offensive player has been forced back to stick distance, the defender now has the upper hand and can begin using stick checks and body position to take away the ball or to force a pass. The basics tools of this are footwork and body position, and the ability to throw simple stick checks such as the poke, slap, and lift. There are other stick checks including the can-opener, helicopter, ice pick, kayak, eggbeater, and (for the highlight reel) the wrap check. But the basics are where every player needs to begin.

Poke Check

The basic poke check is both universal and effective in the game of lacrosse. It is a simple poke of the head of your stick into the controlling hands of the offensive player. It is so ubiquitous because of its simplicity and effectiveness when used properly. Many beginning players target the stick itself for the poke, but it is best to target the hands of the opposing player. The hands present a larger target, and checking them keeps the opposing player from shooting or throwing. In addition, the poke should be delivered without lunging with your body while applying the check. The poke check can be practiced against a pole or against another player holding a stick. Better yet, apply during a two-person slalom drill.

Slap Check

The next basic check is the slap check. This is done using a quick flick of the wrists while again targeting the controlling hands of the offensive player. Many defenders enjoy this check because it is both quick and powerful, and when used in combination with a push or poke check, it can send an offender's stick flying out of his hands. The only thing to watch out for is how you apply it. If you wind up, pulling your stick far back before you apply the check, this will cause most referees to call a slashing penalty. It is best to use quick, axe-like chops that do not disrupt your balance and do not call a referee's attention to the check. Once again, targeting the hands on the stick is best to insure success when using this check.

© Dugald Munro

Lift Check

The lift check is an extremely effective check to use when trying to stop or disrupt an offensive player from throwing or shooting the ball. Indeed, it can even be used on the butt-end of a stick when someone has beaten you to a ground ball. The lift check is applied to the butt-end of the stick or the leading elbow of a player who is in the process of throwing. When the cradle to precradle transition is made, lift the near elbow of the offensive player with the head of your stick. Lifting the elbow impairs the ability of the checked player to rotate his body and causes a bad shot or pass. It is simple to use and extremely effective.

Poke checks	10 right-handed, 10 left-handed
Slap Checks	10 right-handed, 10 left-handed
Lift Check	10 right-handed, 10 left-handed
Combo 1	poke, slap, lift- 10 Right-handed, 10 left-handed
Combo 2	slap, lift, poke- 10 Right-handed, 10 left-handed
Combo 3	lift, slap, poke- 10 Right-handed, 10 left-handed

The challenge when using any stick check is to maintain a good defensive body position and proper balance. Many beginning players stop moving their feet when throwing check, thus freezing themselves in place while attempting to check the stick of an offensive player. It is imperative that defenders learn to keep proper body placement and balance while applying quick and accurate checks. The defender's stick should be used with more finesse and accuracy than brute force and power. In addition, a defender should be able to throw multiple checks in order to set an offensive player up for a takeaway check. Much like a boxer in the ring using his jab to set up a knockout, a defender should watch the reactions of his opponent. If you poke and he pulls his stick back, this sets you up for a slap check. Practicing each individual check against a pole and then practicing throwing combinations is the key. It is very much like a boxer working his punches in combination.

A good drill for multiple checks is the pole drill. Use a standing pole like a heavy bag in a boxing gym. Begin by throwing 10 basic checks with each hand, and then work the combos as described below.

These are just some examples that you can use to develop basic skills before adding impact pushes and hip pokes into the mix. Indeed, one should eventually do all of these drills with both hands and alternating sides to simulate an offensive player in movement. At the highest levels this practice should incorporate one-on-one defense/offense drills as well as two-person slalom drills.

Lift Check

Defensive ground ball skills are not different from general ground ball skills, but place greater emphasis placed upon moving the ball away from the goal itself. A great way to practice this is to play "hockey" with your defense stick. The ability to move and maneuver the ball prior to picking it up is a great defensive skill. In fact, there are some teams that require their long-poles to play field hockey using their lacrosse sticks. If you are a long-pole defensive player, take time to learn how to "dribble" the ball along the ground using the head of your lacrosse pole like a hockey stick. Play forehanded, backhanded, left, and right as well. Develop the skill to "pop" a ball up quickly from the ground and pass it while keeping the head of the stick below knee level. Defensive players can practice this skill and long passes while offensive players are shooting.

PHYSICAL PLAY: HOLDS

Holds are the last aspect of individual defensive skills in which the stick is used. A hold is a legal move that temporarily stops the forward movement of an offensive player. It is usually applied when a defender has lost his or her stick distance and is playing body-to-body against a driving offender. The holds need to be applied quickly to stop a player. Then a push or drop step should be used for the defender to regain position. Holding a player for longer than a second or so will result in a holding penalty. The V-hold is the most common because it keeps the offensive player trapped between your stick and your opposite elbow. Because your d-pole is placed in front of the driving man, this hold can sometimes promote a ward-ing-off move from your opponent, drawing a penalty on him. However, if applied for too long, the V-hold will actually become a true hold, which draws a penalty. It is best to use proper footwork and aggressive checking to keep an offensive player at bay. Hold only as a last resort in order to reposition yourself for a better defensive move.

PHYSICAL PLAY: HITS

There is nothing lacrosse fans love more than the big hits that level an offensive player as he is driving on goal. Indeed, a good legal hit in the game of lacrosse is a thing of beauty. However, a physical game also needs to be a safe game. The rules of lacrosse do offer ample opportunity for hard hits during play, but though a tough and physical game, lacrosse is not football. The goal of a good defenseman is to use the unique tools and skills of the game, sticks and checks, to play solid and exciting defense. If all you see on a lacrosse field is hitting, then you are not watching good lacrosse. Having said that, if you are watching great lacrosse, you will witness to some phenomenal body checks that are both exciting and painful to watch.

The basic rule applying to such physical plays is that a player within 5 yards of the ball is fair game for a legal hit. A legal hit is defined as a hit made with the shoulders against the facing side of an opposing player's body. No hits from behind are allowed. In addition, when hitting you cannot use any part of the stick to apply the hit, and the hit must be made above the waist. For people used to a game such as soccer that avoids player-to-player contact, these rules seem pretty open ended, yet they are designed for exciting play while protecting individual players.

One difference between a lacrosse hit and a football tackle is that a hit in lacrosse is designed as a last resort to stop a player from taking a close range shot or to knock a player off line during a ground ball. It is not meant to knock a player off his feet with the hitter going along for the ride. Indeed, a perfect lacrosse hit would knock an opposing player off line to a ground ball so that a teammate of yours could continue on to pick it up. After a save, it is now the defense that begins the new offensive drive, so it is important that any body check you deliver does not also take you out of the following play action. That is why when practicing body checks it is important to use your opponent's energy against them. Hit just hard enough to effect his performance and not your own. Stay on your feet.

DEFENSIVE DYNAMIC READY POSITION

In addition to the offensive ready position, there is a specific one for defensive play, too. The basic idea is the same. We want to assume a well-balanced athletic position that will allow us to react quickly and easily to any movement of player or ball. The difference is in assuming the defensive position you are not placing the stick in a position to catch and protect the ball, but in a position to check or intercept passes being thrown. In addition, since defensive play is largely reactionary in nature, we are constantly shifting position in relation to the man against whom we are playing rather than playing the ball itself.

To assume the defensive dynamic position, stand with your feet a little wider apart than your shoulders. Your knees are flexed with one foot slightly in front of the other to offer four-way balance. Keep your body weight distributed equally between both your feet. Your head is up and eyes focused on the hips of your opponent. Do not stare directly at the player, for this will cause you to fixate on a single portion of them. Your line-of-sight focus is designed to identify details and not to quickly pick up gross movement like your peripheral vision does. By "soft" focusing on a larger target, the hips or the  numbers on the jersey, you will better be able to pick up movement, thus decreasing the reactionary gap. In addition, looking at the hips allows you to follow the player's body and not be taken in by shoulder, eye, or stick fakes. Lastly, keep your stick pointing directly toward your man and in line with the center of your body. It should be light in your hands but firmly in position so that an offensive player will both see and feel this as a barrier to their progress. By keeping your stick centered and light you will be able to throw checks, be preset for ground balls, and able to lift your stick quickly to intercept or bat down passes.

DEFENSIVE TIPS FROM MATT BROWN

Playing defense just might just be the hardest part of lacrosse. No matter what age you are or how long you have played, defense is a constant education. As a professional lacrosse player, I look at defense as the ability to play one-on-one or man-on-man defense as a basic skill, coming before dealing with team defensive sets or plays. As a player the ability to play one-on-one defense is the base that allows you to develop a consistent and effective team defense. There are many different ways to play defense, and every team has its own way: man-on-man, zone, early slides, late slides, or no slides at all. I personally think that playing a high-pressure defense that will not allow offensive players to easily pass the ball or make plays is the hardest defense to play against. This type of aggressive defense forces the offense to constantly react, not allowing for any setup time or plays to be applied. Being an attackman, I understand a lot of the defensive strategies, and high-pressure, high-risk defense seems to work the best in my book. As a beginning player, focus first on your own ability to play man-on-man defense, and leave it to your coaches to determine team strategies. The better you are as an individual player of defense, the better your team defenses will be.

Hit/Drop/Run Drill

One great drill is the hit/drop/run drill. This drill is to be done with one player or coach holding a tackling shield against his body and a second person standing behind the shield holder. On a signal a defender comes out to make a hit on the shield while the coach or player behind either shoots a ball past the shield holder or drops the ball behind the shield holder, simulating either a shot or ground ball situation. The hitting defender must then react to the ground ball or break out for a clearing pass from the goalie. This is an advanced individual skills drill and should not be performed by beginning or youth players without the supervision of a coach or trainer. Indeed, youth lacrosse coaches should probably not teach such physical play and instead focus on the skills and finesse aspects of the game. Physical play will come as a player moves along in age and physical development. Nevertheless, hitting and body checks are part of the game of lacrosse. Remember that you are playing a game. Keep it safe, keep it fun, and keep it lacrosse.

A SPECIAL NOTE TO GOALIES

It is an accepted fact that any person willing to subject themselves to 100-plus mile an hour shots with a lacrosse ball is simply out of their mind. Goalies are lacrosse's madmen, brave souls who fear no player, feel no pain, and can make or break a team with their play. The true quarterback of the entire squad, goalies are often the best overall players and athletes on the team. They need to have a strategic as well as tactical understanding of the game. They must possess the focus and calmness between the pipes that inspires confidence in their team. They must possess the leadership qualities that allow them to command defenses and initiate offensive drives. With the skills of a hockey goalie and the ability to pass like a quarterback when clearing, the goalie is the last line of defense and the first person to begin an offensive drive once a shot has been stopped.

Due to the specific skills needed, goalies must train above and beyond the scope of this book. However, each and every goalie should possess the skills, agility, strength, and abilities discussed in these pages. In addition, a goalie must have quick reflexes and great vision, possess an in-depth understanding of defensive play, and offensive capability. Though the goalie is often called the last line of defense, he or she is also the beginning of every offensive drive after a successful save has been made.

If you decide to play goalie it is important to seek out good and qualified coaching. Many excellent training camps are available to players as well as DVDs and other resources on the Internet for this specialized position.

Training-wise, it is important to be in as good as or better shape than anyone else on the team. Even though goalkeepers will rarely run the field like middies would, it is important as the leader of the team to condition with your squad so the workout programs in this book apply to you. Beyond that some additional drills and exercises specific to goalies may include: jump rope, juggling, trap shooting, and others.

Goalies should strive to develop all the skills and abilities contained within this book and beyond. It is the author's view that each goalie should have a goalie coach. A person who has spent time between the pipes and can offer the type of advice and training that only experience can give.

CHAPTER 26

STICK TRICKS, FAKES, AND OTHER COOL STUFF

Our generation has seen a revolution in the way lacrosse players train and play. "Old school" lacrosse is being replaced by a new lacrosse culture that, like the skateboard culture, extends beyond the field of play and into our streets and neighborhoods. It is now common to see kids in lacrosse gear walking along the street and practicing in the park. In many homes you now find the clothing, accessories, video games, and websites of the lacrosse fan. Fun stuff like electronic games and off-field practice are shaping the future of the game.

"Stick tricks" is the name that young players give to off-field practice. An incredible diversity of stick tricks are being learned and performed by even the youngest players. Nunchuck-like manipulations of the stick and incredible balancing acts with stick and ball lead up to even more phenomenal, gravity-defying tricks. So advanced are some of these tricks that they have begun, like dribbling tricks in basketball, to find a place on the field. While you will probably not see a player on the field performing a stall catching the ball on the plastic sidewall of his stick, you are likely to see a behind-the-back or between-the-legs pass. Many purist and "old school" coaches look down upon players learning stick tricks, but these skills teach dexterity and sensitivity with the stick and ball. Learning stick tricks is a great way to practice when alone or without a wall to throw against.

Stick tricks also sometimes evolve into necessary skills on the field or in the box. A great example is the behind-the-head pass. In the early days this was considered a showy and disrespectful move, a trick not proper or useful in field play. Now it is a basic skill that every coach expects his or her players to learn. So keep up the creativity, keep up developing new tricks and pushing the envelope of skill development. Who knows, maybe your next trick will become the next invaluable skill for lacrosse greats.

One set of the now-invaluable skills that came from the stick trick games are fakes. Cultivated to the extreme in the indoor version of the game, Canadian indoor players defy the laws of physics with their ability to fake multiple times while driving, dodging, or diving toward the goal. Complicated fakes like the "embarrassing moment" fake are just that to any defender or goalie who falls prey to them. Indeed, stick fakes are now an integral part of the close in offensive game.

As with every skill set in this book, we will begin to use fakes in our other drills and training. For example, before running a slalom drill with a stick in your hand, pull a quick bottom-hand fake on your defender to pull them off line before you hop-switch into a dodge. Or use a top-hand fake when coming off of a split-drill that ends in a one-on-on shot against the goal. Remember that fakes are just one part of your game. Practice them,

cultivate them, and begin to implement them in your practice and games.

There are two basic sticks fakes that you should master first. Both the simple top-hand fake and the bottom-hand fake are spinoffs from your cradling skill. Make sure your cradling is well developed before jumping to fakes.

Top-hand Fake

The top-hand fake is the easiest fake to learn and apply. Made popular by both indoor and outdoor players, the top-hand fake is a quick and simple way to get a reaction from a goalie or a defender. This can give you an offensive edge when driving to the goal or as a predodge set up.

To perform the top-hand fake, begin with your stick in a two handed prethrow hold. Step forward and begin a throwing motion. As you begin to move the stick forward, quickly turn your top hand inward, swiveling the head 180 degrees. This will stop the stick from moving any further forward, and stop the ball from being released from the pocket. Pull your stick back into the ready position and the fake is complete. This fake can be used in myriad situations on the field, the most common being a one-on-one close-in shot on the goalie. A quick top-hand stick fake high and then dropping the ball low works well to fake a goalie out. The top-hand fake can be seen in most games played today, both field and indoor. Practice the top-hand fake with a partner, against the wall, or better yet in a mirror to see how effective it is. Remember to practice this fake with both left and right hands. Make sure to use quick short movements while also allowing your eyes and body to "sell it." You will find that it is a fast and short movement that can work wonders on the field.

Bottom-hand Fake

The bottom-hand fake is a little more complicated and takes more skill to perform. In addition it can be made more difficult, or even impossible, if your mesh is not strung properly. In order to be able to pull off a great bottom-hand fake, your stick needs to have some hold. Maybe this is why the bottom-hand is predominantly seen in the indoor box version of the game, where sticks can have pockets so deep that a player actually has to work to get the ball out of his stick. Nevertheless, the bottom-hand fake is effective on the field of play and is best used when trying to outposition a defender who is playing too far off. It is a great predodge fake and, when done with speed and full range of motion, can fake an entire defensive unit out of their socks.

To perform a bottom-hand fake, begin in the ready position. Step forward and begin the throwing motion. As the stick comes forward, twist the bottom wrist to the outside. Let the head of the stick turn 180 degrees, stopping the ball from releasing. Bring the stick back to the ready position to complete the fake. Depending on the hold of your pocket, this fake can be thrown at the end of a full extension of a passing move or even a shot. Practice this fake with a friend, against a wall, and in the mirror, using both your right and left hand.

Other Fakes

Along with stick fakes lacrosse players can use body fakes, eye fakes, voice fakes, and arm fakes. Each has its place in the differing versions of the game. An example of a body fake is the rocker fake. This is when you drive against a defender who begins a hold on you as you drive to the goal. Feel the direction of the push or hold move counter to that pressure and raising your stick high to bait a check. As the check comes, rock back to the other direction, dropping your stick down low for a sidearm or underhand shot. An eye fake can be very effective if done properly. The eye fake is executed when you turn your head to look at a teammate but throw to another teammate who is not directly in your line of sight. A voice fake is when you make a pass to someone while simultaneously calling out the number, name, or position of a different teammate. This technique is typically considered unsportsmanlike conduct in youth and high school lacrosse, but in the boxes and fields of men's club play, it is a standard. The teeter-totter is an example of an arm fake in which you raise your leading elbow so that it looks like you will shoot high, and then you quickly drop your stick down for a low shot.

These are just a few examples of the literally hundreds of fakes that exist in the game of lacrosse and that will continue to evolve with the game as subtle skills and abilities that give the individual player an edge. In the increased crosspollination of indoor box and outdoor field skills these types of techniques will become hallmarks of the highest level of play. In fact, it is already being seen on the fields of major league lacrosse, where the new shot clock rules and the incredible diversity of skill has created a new version of lacrosse that combines the excitement of the outdoor game with the technical skills of box lacrosse.

National Lacrosse League game with the Philadelphia Wings visiting the Minnesota Swarm at the Xcel Energy Center, St. Paul, Minnesota.

CONCLUSION BY MATT BROWN

IN HIS OWN WORDS, BY MATT BROWN

Lacrosse is the complete sport. It has the speed of hockey, the hitting of football, the excitement of basketball, and the endurance of soccer all in one. For me, lacrosse is not just a job, it is a passion. Like all top-level players, I have put my time in on practice field, in the gym, and in the film room. Always my goal is to shape myself into the best player I can possibly be. Every week I push myself hard to become a better player.

As a child growing up in Burnaby, British Columbia, Canada, I began playing lacrosse when I was 7 years old. Lacrosse in Burnaby has always been a very competitive sport. A lot of great players, past and present, have come through Burnaby's youth lacrosse system. Every year it was a real challenge to make the team and to be the best player I could be. After playing in the minors, I was able at the age of 15 to go to Junior A-level lacrosse for the Burnaby Lakers. I played six seasons for them, making it to the Minto Cup, the junior national finals, every year. We were fortunate enough to win three Minto Cups along with a number of individual player awards.

Because of hard work and an ability to excel in the game, I was fortunate enough to earn a four-year lacrosse scholarship to the University of Denver. I was one of the first students from Western Canada to receive a scholarship for lacrosse in Division 1 school. I played 4 years at Denver, leading the team in scoring every year. I began my freshman year with a school record, seven straight hat tricks, and finished fourth in the all-time scoring. I felt that it was a great honor to be able to play the sport while obtaining an education. I graduated with a degree in finance and marketing.

After my time at the University of Denver, I was very happy to be afforded the opportunity to continue playing lacrosse. I was drafted fifth overall by the Arizona Sting, an indoor National Lacrosse League team. I played in all 16 regular season games, plus two playoff games, in my inaugural year (2006). Over the season I accumulated 19 goals and 21 assists for a total of 40 points. In addition, I was recruited to play in outdoor Major League Lacrosse as a member of the Denver Outlaws. Currently, I split my time between Colorado and Arizona, playing and promoting the great sport of lacrosse. I am fortunate enough to be able to play professionally in the indoor leagues, a great honor as a Canadian national, and in the outdoor leagues, reflecting my American attachment to the game. Besides playing, I travel the country promoting the game through lacrosse camps and training clinics. It is a passion for me, as I have said, and it will continue to be a driving force in my life. I play it not because of money, not because of fame, but because I love the sport. It is the ultimate sport, and whether you are a fan, parent, player, or coach, I want to improve your knowledge and skills in the game I love. Lacrosse is the fastest-growing sport in the United States for a reason, and I am proud to be part of that incredible growth, now and into the future.

—Matt Brown

APPENDIX A

BASIC LACROSSE SKILLS TEST

Prior to jumping into this program, it is important that you set goals that can be realistically achieved. In general, the goal is to improve speed, agility, skills, and strength. In order to measure improvement, your skills must be tested and quantified. Performing the Basic Lacrosse Physical Fitness and Skills test does this. Unlike a general PT test, this is lacrosse-specific and will allow you to begin to log your achievements in the basic skills areas. For more advanced players, this quantification and testing of your base abilities will be a valuable gauge of your progress in training as well as a tool for potential recruitment at the high school, college, and pro levels. Indeed, getting habituated to tests of this nature are a must for any player wishing to play at the highest levels. The basic Lacrosse Physical Fitness and Skills test is as follows:

PART 1: SKILLS

This section helps to quantify your ability in the basic lacrosse skills: ground balls, passing, catching, dodging, and shooting.

Ground Balls

This basic test examines a player's ability to pick up ground balls while on the run, an important part of playing the game. It also allows a coach or player to observe any mistake in form or technique under pressure of the clock. To perform the test, place six lacrosse balls on the ground about 12 inches apart.

Begin 10 yards away from the ball on the ground and spring toward the balls, dropping down to pick up a ground ball as you go by. Run past the balls to a point 10 yards beyond, drop the ball you have picked up, and run back to the ground balls again. Continue to run back and forth until each of the groundballs has been picked up. Make sure to pick up three with your right hand and three with your left. Record your time and log any missed ground balls.

Passing and Catching

This test examines a player's ability to throw and catch on the run. This drill necessitates two administrators, six balls, and the player himself. Have a player face a feeder about 10 yards away. The feeder will throw a ball to the player who is running toward the feeder, who must then catch the pass and perform a turn to the outside so that they are now facing away from the feeder. The player must then make a pass to a second test administrator who is standing anywhere from 8-15 yards away. After the pass is made to the second man, the player will then curve back toward the feeder for another ball. As this is happening, the second administrator is changing their position on the field. Continue this for six compete catches and passes, being sure to perform three left-handed and three right-handed. Make sure the second administrator keeps moving so that the passing distances vary. When testing long-pole defenders the pass distances should be increased up to 40 yards. Record time of performance and log any missed passes or catches.

Dodging

This test examines the players' ability to perform the basic dodges and evasive moves in lacrosse while protecting the stick. The dodging test is relatively simple to perform. Set up a runway about 20 yards long, and set cones along this path, placing one every 5 yards. Now have the player sprint to the first cone and perform a face dodge, split dodge, or roll dodge at each cone until he is through all five. Record time of performance and any dropped balls or missed dodges.

Shooting

This test examines the player's ability to shoot the ball with speed and accuracy under pressure. The shooting test involves six balls and three shooting stations on each side of the goal. The first shooting station should be 3-5 yards from the goal, the second 8-10 yards, and the third 12-15 yards. Have a player begin running to the near post position and feed a pass to them. The player then performs a quick stick shot and then turns to the outside to be fed again from the opposite side of the goal. This continues moving out to the second shooting station, where a quick wrist shot should be taken. The third station should be a strong crank shot from outside. Novice players should have the entire goal to shoot at while advanced players should shoot against a goalie or a shooting target. Record time of performance, missed shots, and if possible, speed of each shot.

Combination

This final test completes the skills exam by combining each skill into one drill. Have a player begin

at the midfield line. Set up a ground ball halfway to the restraining line, a cone just inside the restraining line, and a second administrator at a low post position at either side of the goal. Have the player sprint to the ground ball and pick it up, then perform a dodge at the cone, then pass to the administrator, then have the player keep running and receive a pass back from the administrator, finishing in a moving shot on goal. Record time of performance, log any missed ground balls, dodges, passes, dropped balls, and speed and placement of shot. Perform this both left- and right-handed.

PART 2- FITNESS

This is the second phase of the exam that tests lacrosse fitness levels.

40-yard Sprint

This test examines a player's raw running speed unencumbered by equipment or stick. This is a simple timed sprint for maximum speed. Record time of performance.

40 with stick and ball

This test examines a player's ability to translate raw running speed into a game situation while encumbered with full equipment and stick. This is also a simple sprint but now with full pads, stick, and a ball in the stick. Record time of performance and log any dropped balls.

Slalom run

This test examines a player's ability to maneuver and run while quickly changing direction, as you would do in a game. Set up a slalom ladder as described in the agility section of this book. Have the player perform a full-speed slalom run with at least six position changes over 20 yards. Record time of performance.

220

This tests a player's cardiovascular fitness level. This is a 220-yard run for max speed. Record time of performance.

Turkish Get-Ups

This test examines players' anaerobic conditioning and functional strength. Using a kettlebell or dumbbell perform as many Turkish get-ups as possible in 3 minutes. Be sure to alternate hands. Record number of performance.

Record your results of this exam, and find a time to retest once every month or so to see your progress. It is also beneficial to use a video camera, which will also let you see your skill-based progress as a third party observer. This way you can watch your form and see any technical mistakes that may need to be corrected. Do not get overly concerned with your initial performance or the performance of your teammates. This is a gauge for you only to see how well you progress through the upcoming training season.

LEGENDS OF THE GAME AND STARS

When it comes to individual players there is one name that transcend both indoor and field lacrosse. It is one of the few names from that is often familiar to those who know little or nothing about lacrosse. That name is Gait. Gary and Paul Gait are the identical twin brothers who hand-in hand revolutionized the sport of lacrosse. Born on April 5, 1967 in Victoria, British Columbia, the powerhouse twins picked up lacrosse as an inexpensive alternative to Canada's second national sport, hockey. At over 6 feet tall and 200-plus pounds of natural athleticism, the Gaits began a revolution in lacrosse. With their size, speed, and agility was added exceptional abilities with the stick and a creative approach to playing the game. They developed new ways in which to score including the infamous, and now illegal, "Air Gait" in which a player drives from behind the goal and jumps out and over the crease to shoot while in midair. Like the first slamdunk in basketball it marked a moment that would forever change the way the sport was played. Shocking to those not familiar with such aggressive and creative moves, yet exhilarating just the same. As lacrosse purists looked on, the Gait's took hold off the game and changed it forever.

GAIT BROTHERS

The Gait name is synonymous with lacrosse. As the originators of spectacular moves on the field such as the legendary "Air Gait," the athletic twins from Canada teamed up to revolutionize the sport. As members of their college team they helped Syracuse to win three straight NCAA titles from 1988-90. Gary Gait was a four-time All-American and selected as the National Player of the Year in 1988 and 1990. Paul Gait was a three-time All-American and MVP of the 1989 championship game against Johns Hopkins. Both players were named to the NCAA's 25th Anniversary Lacrosse Team in 1997. In 2006 both Paul and Gary were voted into the National Lacrosse League Hall of Fame.

Paul Gait's honors in lacrosse are legendary and include:

- First-team All-America honors from 1988 to 1990 at Syracuse.
- NCAA Tournament's Most Outstanding Player in 1989.
- USILA North–South All-Star Game in 1990.
- Member of the Canadian National Team in the ILF World Championships in 1990, 1994, 1998 and 2002.
- All-World recognition in 1994.
- National Lacrosse League, and its predecessor indoor leagues from 1991 to 2005, earning the NLL's MVP award in 2002.

- Eight-time first-team All-Pro and three-time second-team All-Pro in the NLL.
- He also played outdoor post-collegiate club lacrosse and earned multiple honors.
- 2001, he helped the Long Island Lizards capture the inaugural Major League Lacrosse championships.
- Lacrosse Magazine named him to its All-twentieth Century Team and the NCAA named him to its 25th Anniversary Team.

Paul Gait's accomplishments on the field of lacrosse are eclipsed only in greatness by his identical twin Gary, who has been called the Michael Jordan of lacrosse. One of the greatest lacrosse players ever, Gary Gaits' accomplishments include:

- First-team All-America honors three times at Syracuse University.
- USILA player of the year honors twice in leading Syracuse to national championships in 1988, 1989 and 1990.
- Numerous NCAA records, including goals scored in a tournament game, single tournament, and career tournaments.
- Gait remains Syracuse's all-time leading goal scorer with 192, and he was named to the 1990 USILA North-South Game.
- Member of the Canadian National Team in the ILF World Championships in 1990, 1994, and 1998, earning a place on the All-World Team each year.
- 1991 he began a 15-year professional indoor career, winning Rookie of the Year honors.
- 15-time All-Pro and six-time MVP of the National Lacrosse League.
- Ranked as the NLL's all-time leading goal and points scorer (until 2006).

- Played in Major League Lacrosse since the league's inception in 2001, helping the Baltimore Bayhawks to league championships in 2002 and 2005 as a player-coach.
- 10 years in the USCLA, winning its MVP award four times and its championship twice.
- Assistant coach on the University of Maryland women's teams that won seven consecutive NCAA championships in the 1990s and early 2000s.
- *Lacrosse Magazine* named him to its All-twentieth Century Team.
- NCAA named him to its 25th Anniversary Team.
- Head coach of the NLL's Colorado Mammoth
- 2006 Winner of NLL championship as Coach of the Mammoth.

Paul and Gary Gait continue to promote the sport of lacrosse, though in two different ways. Gary has recently retired as a player and has begun to make his mark as a coach for both the NLL's Colorado Mammoth and MLL's Baltimore Bayhawks. Paul Gait has been a driving force in the development of cutting-edge lacrosse equipment as member of DeBeer/Gait Lacrosse. His innovative designs are shaping the future of the game. Together, the most well-known name in lacrosse is continuing to make its mark on future generations of players.

THE POWELLS

Another famous lacrosse family is the Powells, Casey, Ryan, and Mikey. The Powell name is well known in the world of lacrosse, and much of what they have accomplished as outstanding college and pro players is legendary. All three brothers have carved their names in stone when playing for Syracuse University and even more so in their postcollegiate careers while helping to improve the game of lacrosse nationwide. Known for their fierce competitiveness and distinctly different styles of play, the brothers Powell have taken up where the Gaits left off in moving the sport to a new and more professional level.

The story begins with the first of the three brothers, Casey, and his superb and fierce style of play with the Orange of Syracuse. His achievements include:

- NCAA Player of the Year (1997 and 1998)
- Attackman of the Year (1997, 1998)
- Syracuse University all-time leading scorer
- Four-time MLL All-Star
- Two-time NLL All-Star (Anaheim)
- MLL all-time leading scorer (2001, 2002)
- Member of Team USA in World Team Competition
- NCAA Championship with Syracuse
- World Championship with Team USA
- MLL Championship (Long Island Lizards)

As a true ambassador for lacrosse, he has spent the last 7 years traveling the world to promote the sport. As a co-owner of Powell Brother's Lacrosse Camps, Casey gets to speak at numerous lacrosse clinics and seminars throughout the world, teaching the next generation of champions the spirit of the game. Casey has used his fame as a player to give back to the community as well, getting involved in a variety of charity and community events, most notably the "Powell Warriors" to help increase awareness in the fight against cancer.

The next in the line of Powells is Ryan, considered one of the best field lacrosse players in the world today. His enthusiasm and passion for the game is evident every time he steps onto the field. Another alum of the lacrosse dynasty called Syracuse University, Ryan's career stats include:

- Four-time NCAA All-American
- 2000 NCAA Player of the Year
- 2000 Attackmen of the Year

Tied his brother Casey's record as SU's leading scorer in his last game while winning the 2000 Division 1 Championship

- Three-time Major League Lacrosse All-Star
- All-Time Leading Scorer for Rochester Rattlers
- 2001 MLL League Leading Scorer and league MVP

Along with his brothers, Ryan is co-owner of the Powell Brother's Camps and spends much of his time traveling to various lacrosse clinics every year. In addition Ryan has begun to coach in order to give back to the sport he so loves. In 2004 he served as assistant coach for Syracuse University's NCAA Division 1 Championship team. Currently, he is the head coach at Mullen High School in Colorado, an up-and-coming powerhouse of high school lacrosse.

The third brother, Mikey, is considered by many to be the best player of the three. Not as large and powerful as his formidable brothers, his natural athleticism and incredible agility and speed have taken this 165-pounder to the pinnacle of lacrosse excellence. Following the family tradition, Mickey also attended Syracuse where his exploits on the field, including a front-flip dodge while holding the ball, made him a legend. His accomplishments include:

- Broke his brothers' shared record as the university's all-time leading scorer
- Four-time NCAA Division 1 first team All-American honors
- Four-time Jack Turnbull Awards for division 1 attackman of the year, the first to do so since it began in 1946
- Received Lt. Raymond Enners Award as the Player of the Year in college lacrosse as a senior Tewaaraton finalist each of his 4 years and won the award in 2002 and 2004
- NCAA Championship in 2004 with Casey in the stands and Ryan on the sideline

GLOSSARY

ATTACKMAN: Forward offensive position in attack that plays proximate to the goal and must stay on the offensive side of the field at all times.

ATTACK GOAL AREA: The area defined by a line drawn sideline-to-sideline 20 yards from the face of the goal. Once the offensive team crosses the midfield line, it has 10 seconds to move the ball into its attack goal area.

ARM GUARD: Protective piece of equipment worn to protect against checks.

BAGATAWAY: Native American name for lacrosse.

BEHIND-THE-HEAD PASS: A former stick trick turned lacrosse staple, it is a method of passing the ball behind your head to another player.

BODY CHECK: Contact with an opponent from the front (between the shoulders and waist) when the opponent has the ball or is within 5 yards of a loose ball.

BOX: An area used to hold players who have been served with penalties, and through which substitutions "on the fly" are permitted directly from the sideline onto the field.

BOX LACROSSE: The indoor version of the sport played on turf-covered hockey rinks. It is the national sport of Canada. Played in the United States as a club sport and the professional indoor lacrosse league known as the National Lacrosse League (NLL).

BRINE: Major lacrosse equipment manufacturer.

BUTT-END: The bottom part of a lacrosse shaft that by rule must be covered with tape or some form of endcap for protection.

CANADIAN: A citizen of Canada and a player of box lacrosse. Also a method of throwing from your off-hand side by using a cross-body method.

CATCHING: The act of receiving a passed ball with the stick.

CHECKING: The act of attempting to dislodge the ball from an opponent's stick.

CHECK-UP: A call given by the goalie to tell each defender to find his man and call out his number.

CLAMP: A face-off maneuver executed by quickly pushing the back of the stick on top of the ball.

CLEARING: Running or passing the ball from the defensive half of the field to the attack goal area.

CRADLING: The coordinated motion of the arms and wrists that keeps the ball secure in the pocket and ready to be passed or shot when running.

CRANK: A hard shot from the outside.

CREASE: A circle around the goal with a radius of 9 feet into which only defensive players may enter.

CROSSE (STICK): The equipment used to throw, catch, and carry the ball.

CROSS CHECK: An illegal check in which a player hits an opposing player with the shaft of the lacrosse stick. A dangerous and illegal play in field lacrosse and a penalty. A common and legal move in box.

CUTTING: A movement by an offensive player without the ball, toward the opponent's goal, in anticipation of a feed and shot.

DeBEER: Lacrosse equipment manufacturer that produces the majority of women's lacrosse equipment. See also Gait.

DEFENSIVE CLEARING AREA: The area defined by a line drawn sideline-to-sideline 20 yards from the face of the goal. Once the defensive team gains possession of the ball in this area, it has 10 seconds to move the ball across the midfield line.

DEFENSEMAN: A player who is assigned to aid in protecting offensive players from scoring on the goal through physical play, checks, and body positioning. In box lacrosse they are substituted out on the fly when offensive players come off the turf; in field they are to remain on the defensive side of the field at all times.

DEHUNTSHIGWA'ES: "Lacrosse" in Onondaga, a Native North American tribe.

D-POLE: A field lacrosse defenseman's stick, unique in its length of between 52-72 inches.

DIP AND DUNK: A move used when one-on-one with the goalie in close proximity to the goal. It used a top-hand fake while dropping your body low and shooting the ball high. A favorite move of the Powell brothers.

DODGE: The footwork and running moves used to move past a defenseman while driving to the goal. Off-ball dodging is also used to "get open" for a pass.

EXTRA MAN OFFENSE (EMO): A man advantage that results from a timeserving penalty.

FACE OFF: A technique used to put the ball in play at the start of each quarter or after a goal is scored. The players squat down and the ball is placed between their crosses.

FAST BREAK: A transition scoring opportunity in which the offense has at least a one-man advantage.

FEEDING: Passing the ball to a teammate who is in position for a shot on goal.

GAIT LACROSSE: Equipment company founded by Paul Gait.

GROUND BALL: A loose ball on the playing field.

HANDLE (SHAFT): An aluminum, wooden, or composite pole connected to the head of the crosse.

HARROW: A major lacrosse equipment supplier specializing in shafts made from composite materials.

HEAD: The plastic or wood part of the stick connected to the handle.

INSIDE LACROSSE MAGAZINE: The major lacrosse periodical.

LACROSSE MAGAZINE: Official magazine of US Lacrosse, America's sanctioning body for lacrosse.

LIFT CHECK: A check delivered to the leading elbow of an offensive player when attempting to shoot that is performed by lifting their elbow with the head of the stick.

MAN DOWN DEFENSE (MDD): The situation that results from a timeserving penalty that causes the defense to play with at least a one-man disadvantage.

MAJOR LEAGUE LACROSSE: The American professional lacrosse league that plays field lacrosse in the summer months.

MIDFIELD LINE: The line that bisects the field of play.

MIDFIELDER: A roaming player who plays both offense and defense and is responsible for the transition portion of the game, they are called the workhorses of lacrosse.

MOHAWK INTERNATIONAL LACROSSE: One of the oldest lacrosse stick manufacturing companies in the world located on the Akesane reservation where both modern plastic heads and traditional all-wood sticks are still produced. Official stick of the National Lacrosse League.

NATIONAL LACROSSE LEAGUE: Canadian/American indoor professional lacrosse league.

ON-THE-FLY SUBSTITUTION: A substitution made during play.

PASSING: The act of throwing the ball to a teammate with the crosse.

PICK: An offensive maneuver in which a stationary player attempts to block the path of a defender guarding another offensive player.

POCKET: The strung part of the head of the stick that holds the ball.

POKE CHECK: A stick check in which the player pokes the head of his stick at an opponent's stick through the top hand by pushing with the bottom hand.

RAKE: A face-off move in which a player sweeps the ball to the side.

RIDING: The act of trying to prevent a team from clearing the ball.

RELEASE: The term used by an official to notify a penalized player in the box that he may re-enter the game.

SCREENING: An offensive tactic in which a player near the crease positions himself so as to block the goalkeeper's view of the ball.

SCOOPING: The act of picking up a loose ball with the crosse.

SHAMROCK LACROSSE: Lacrosse equipment manufacturer.

SHOOTING: The act of throwing the ball with the crosse toward the goal in an attempt to score.

SLAP CHECK: A stick check in which a player slaps the head of his stick against his opponent's stick.

STX: A major lacrosse equipment manufacturer.

TEKWAARATHON: Native American (Mohawk) name for lacrosse. Also the name of the trophy given to the best player in the collegiate ranks. It is the Heismann of lacrosse.

UNSETTLED SITUATION: Any situation in which the defense is not positioned correctly, usually due to a loose ball or broken clear.

US LACROSSE: US based sanctioning body for lacrosse.

WARRIOR LACROSSE: Major lacrosse equipment manufacturer.

WRAP CHECK: A one-handed check in which the defender swings his stick around his opponent's body to dislodge the ball. (This check is only legal at the highest level of play.)

APPENDIX D

REFERENCES

Arthur, Michael, and Bailey, Bryan. *Complete Conditioning for Football*. Human Kinetics Publishers: 1998, Champaign, IL.

Baggett, Kelly. *"The Best Exercises for Developing Speed and Vertical Jump."* http://www.higher-faster-sports.com/jumphigher.html

Baggett, Kelly. *"Plyometric Training for the Upper Body."* http://www.bodybuilding .com/fun/kelly7.htm

Cisco, Peter, and Little, John R. *Power Factor Training: A Scientific Approach to Building Lean Muscle Mass*. McGraw-Hill: 1997, New York, NY.

Croxdale, Kenny, and Morris, Tom. *"Plyometric Bench Press Training for More Strength and Power."* http://www.strengthcats.com/plyobenchpress.htm

Goldstein, Yuval. *"Practical Application of Speed Training Techniques in Advanced Bodybuilding Training."* http://www.mesomorphosis.com/articles/goldstein/speed-training.htm

Nawrocki, Nolan. *"Evolutionary Training: Archuleta explodes past his competition."* http://archive.profootball-weekly.com/content/archives2001/features_2001/nawrocki_061901.asp

Schwarzenegger, Arnold and Dobbins, Bill. *The New Encyclopedia of Modern Bodybuilding*. Simon and Schuster: 1999, New York, NY.

Verstegen, Mark and Williams, Pete. *Core Performance: The Revolutionary Workout Program to Transform Your Body and Your Life*. Rodale Books, 2005: New York, NY.

ADDITIONAL WEB RESOURCES

BCLacrosse.com
The British Columbia Lacrosse Association

InsideLacrosse.com
The website of the popular magazine *InsideLacrosse*

Lacrosse.ca
The Canadian Lacrosse Association, also in French

Laxlocker.com
An Arizona-based youth league

NLL.com
The National League Lacrosse

NSCA.com
The National Strength and Conditioning
Association

MajorLeagueLacrosse.com
The Major League Lacrosse

www.USLacrosse.org
US Lacrosse's homepage

Vincent Perez-Mazzola is a youth and high school lacrosse coach and is a fitness trainer for professional athletes in lacrosse, hockey, professional boxing and mixed martial arts. Vincent played during high school in Monterey, California, college at George Washington University, and now plays in recreational adult indoor and outdoor leagues. He resides in Fountain Hills, Arizona.

Jamie Munro has been the Head Coach for Men's Lacrosse at the University of Denver for seven years. During his tenure, he led the Pioneers to a five-game winning streak, the longest in Denver history at the Division I level, and has claimed top honors in the Great Western Lacrosse League (GWLL) (along with Notre Dame and The Ohio State). Munro holds the record for leading the Pioneers to the most wins (a 43-38 overall record in six seasons) and aided in the transition to Division I. Prior to taking the reins of the Pioneer program, Munro spent eight seasons as the top assistant coach at Yale, and in his final year, assumed the team's defensive coordinator role.

Munro is also the founder of Run and Shoot Lacrosse, a nationwide program that operates summer camps for young players. He also helped develop the USA Lacrosse Progression, a five-step approach to teaching and learning the game. The program has been featured in the magazine Lacrosse and was turned into a video series in 1997.

As a player, Munro was a four-year member of the Brown University lacrosse team, garnering All-Ivy League honors from 1987-89 and capped his collegiate career by earning All-America status in 1989. Munro captained the Bears' squad as a senior and played in the North-South College All-Star Game in 1989. Munro also played professionally for the Boston Blazers of the Major Indoor Lacrosse League and was named to the USILA Club all-star team in 1993.

Matt Brown is a professional lacrosse player for the National Lacrosse League team the Arizona Sting and the Major League Lacrosse team the Denver Outlaws. In the 2006 season, he became the MLL's lead goal scorer with 38 goals in 11 games. He is also the assistant coach at the University of Denver, and during his collegiate career there, tallied 137 points (113G-24A) in 56 games. He ranks fourth all-time in goals scored for the Pioneers and has earned numerous accolades for his play in 2005, including First Team All-GWLL at attack, Preseason All-America Honorable Mention Honors, GWLL Player of the Week honors on April 12, and Pioneer Face-off Classic All-tournament team honors at attack.

(Photo used by permission of the University of Denver Athletics Media Relations.)

INDEX

THE LACROSSE TRAINING BIBLE

L

Lacrosse World Games, 7
lactate theshold training, 133
ladders and slalom, 57
lateral raise, 77
learning lacrosse, 18-19
leg press, 84
lift, 220
lift check, 224-225, 244
little bear runs, 132
Livingston, Jessica, 12

M

Major Indoor Lacrosse League, 8
Major League Lacrosse (MLL), 9, 244
man down defense (MDD), 244
max heart rate, calculating, 129
medicine ball push ups, 110
medicine ball runs, 132
medicine ball twists, 112
men's field lacrosse, 14
mesh, 31-33
midfield, 17
midfield line, 244
midfielder, 245
military press, 83
modern game, 5-6
Mohawk International Lacrosse, 4, 245
Montreal Lacrosse Club, 4
Morrow, Dave, 9
Munroe, Jamie, 18

N

National Lacrosse League, 6, 8-9, 245
Native American origins, 3-4
neck rotations, 40
nutrition
    carbohydrates, 22-23
    eating guidelines, 24-25
    electrolytes, 29
    fat, 23-24
    glutamine, 28
    hydration, 27
    pre-training/game eating, 26-27
    protein, 23, 29
    role of, 22
    sample diet, 25-26
    supplements, nutritional, 27-29
    Vitamin C, 28

Vitamin E, 28-29
zinc, 29

O

on-the-fly substitution, 245
one-handed cradle, 151, 152-153
one-handed fielding, 160
one-legged deadlift, 98
one-legged lateral raises, 108
one-legged reaches, 114
one-legged towel squat, 115
overhand shooting, 207
overhand throw, 179
overhead push-press, 88
overhead squat, 107

P

pads and protective equipment, 35-36
passing, 236, 245
    overview, 185-186
    tips, 186
    wall ball, playing, 188
performance enhancement drugs, 29-30
physio-ball press, 97
physio-ball push-ups, 85, 116
physio-ball twists, 109
pick, 245
pick-up stick drill, 163
plyo-push-ups, 95
pocket, 245
poke, 220
poke check, 221, 245
positions, 16-18
postseason recovery, 126, 134
Powell, Casey, 18, 240-241
Powell, Mikey, 240, 241, 242
Powell, Ryan, 240, 241
power cradle, 151
pre-training/game eating, 26-27
preseason balance program, 122-123
preseason conditioning session (balance), 130, 132
preseason conditioning session (explosive), 130
preseason conditioning session (strength), 129-130
preseason explosive program, 120-121
preseason strength program, 118
prethrow, 158
professional lacrosse leagues, 7
protein, 23, 29
pull-ups, 113

R

rake, 245
reach back/bend forward, 137
recovery shake recipe, 27
release, 245
release point, 202
renegade rows, 101
riding, 245
1RM, calculating, 74
Robertson, Tim, 9
rocker fake, 232
roll dodge, 196
rows, 80

S

220's, 132, 238
scooping, 245
scorpions, 48, 142
screening, 245
shaft, 33, 244
shooting, 237, 245
   body positioning, 203
   drills, 206
   face-away ball throw, 204
   follow through and focus, 205
   fresh balls *vs.* potatoes, 205
   overhand shooting, 207
   overview, 200, 202
   release point, 202
   shooting drill, 208-209
   tips, 209
shooting drill, 208-209
shoulder rotations, 41
side bends, 138
sidearm throw, 181
skips, 52
slalom run, 237
slalom run (version one), 62
slalom run (version two), 64
slap, 220
slap check, 222, 245
split dodge, 194
split drill, 66
squats, 78, 79
Steinfeld, Jake, 9
steroids, anabolic, 29-30
stick, 31, 243
stick position, 190

stick position and the cross-body scoop, 166
stick tricks, 230
stimulants, 29
strength training
   alternate hanging leg raises, 100
   alternating one-legged squat-sits, 111
   back extensions, 82
   barbell snatch, 94
   barbell twists, 89
   bench press, 76
   bottom bench, 91
   bottom squats, 90
   breathing exercises, 73
   cable twists, 96
   components of, 72
   crunches, 117
   deadlift, 81
   dumbbell cleans, 103
   dumbbell squat press, 102
   equipment, 73
   hanging cleans, 92
   hanging leg raises, 86
   jerks, 93
   kettlebell snatch, 106
   lateral raise, 77
   leg press, 84
   medicine ball push ups, 110
   medicine ball twists, 112
   military press, 83
   one-legged deadlift, 98
   one-legged lateral raises, 108
   one-legged reaches, 114
   one-legged towel squat, 115
   overhead push-press, 88
   overhead squat, 107
   physio-ball press, 97
   physio-ball push-ups, 85
   physio-ball push-ups, 116
   physio-ball twists, 109
   plyo-push-ups, 95
   pull-ups, 113
   renegade rows, 101
   1RM, calculating, 74
   rows, 80
   squats, 78, 79
   Turkish get-up, 99
   twisting hyperextensions, 104, 105
   weighted pull-ups, 87
stretching, dangers of, 39